Reader Reviews

A company's most important asset is its people, in particular, those with the greatest experience. If these employees look to their futures with more certainty, they will be more focused and engaged in their current jobs and be able to transition more smoothly into the retirement they deserve. Your Retirement Quest is a pathway toward that more certain future, helping to both envision the future and then plan it.

Richard Antoine
Global Human Resources Officer, Retired, Procter & Gamble

This book demystifies the obstacles that stand in the way of a fulfilling retirement. Anyone interested in creating a long-lasting impact by giving back should read Your Retirement Quest.

Tom Bloch
Former CEO, H&R Block
Co-founder, University Academy, Kansas City public charter school
Author, *Stand for the Best*

The emphasis by Lawrence and Spector on lifelong growth and connectedness is right on target. This is par' ''' true when we are in our 50s, 60s and beyond. The OLLI an   learning programs at many U.S. colleges focus on both   *nind and expanding social opportunities.* Your Retirem   *ines hard facts and anecdotes to encourage readers to e*   *; by being fully alive.*

Tom Noonan
Board Chair, Osher Lifelong Learning Institute   icinnati
CEO (retired), The Community Press, Inc.

This book provides timely guidance not only for those approaching retirement but anyone preparing to pursue a good life now. The authors strike an unusual Golden Mean: they help readers engage in deep self-reflection on the core questions of life and also provide the practical tools for fulfillment.

Laura Nash, PhD
Former Senior Lecturer, Harvard Business School
Co-author: *Just Enough: Tools for Creating Success in Your Work and Life*

My personal family experiences taught me I need to make every day count. My business experiences taught me that I need to keep learning and help others around me do the same. My retirement years have taught me that I have the opportunity to live my dreams and give back to others. I am excited about Your Retirement Quest, *because it teaches what I have learned.*

Greg Lawton
President and CEO (retired), JohnsonDiversey, Inc.

While in my business, financial security is a focus, it is good to see a practical approach to the other aspects of living a successful retirement. Your Retirement Quest *puts financial security in its proper perspective, important, but not the key to happiness. I found the model Spector and Lawrence use to describe what it takes to live a fulfilling retirement very helpful; especially as I look forward to that phase of my life.*

Jane Brauer, PhD
Senior Director of Research,
Bank of America Merrill Lynch Securities

Our program, "Every Child Succeeds," is successful, in large part, because of the retirees who volunteer to give of their time, energy, and compassion to help our families. In Your Retirement Quest, *Keith and Alan have created a powerful framework to think about a meaningful retirement and have correctly identified "giving back" as one of the important critical factors—our client families, our community, and our volunteers all benefit from "giving back."*

Judith Van Ginkel, PhD
President, Every Child Succeeds
Author, *Life Begins and Ends with Girlfriends*

I have had the pleasure of serving as an advisor to retirees, with all levels of net worth, for over 25 years. Those who seem happiest and most fulfilled successfully budget both their money and their time. Lawrence and Spector accurately convey this truth in Your Retirement Quest— *financial security is important, but it is only one of the many factors that influence retirement life. I recommend this book to anyone planning for retirement or looking for ways to enhance their current retirement lifestyle. As their chapter title says, "It's Not All about the Money."*

Dan Kiley
President, Retirement Corporation of America
Founder, Retirement University

I have had the privilege of seeing firsthand what is important to successfully transition from a career to a healthy and fulfilling life. There are many dimensions to doing this and Your Retirement Quest *provides invaluable insights and a roadmap to guide us on this journey.*

Doug Spitler
President and CEO, Episcopal Retirement Homes

Baby Boomers are retiring and entering unfamiliar territory. Your Retirement Quest *authors Alan Spector and Keith Lawrence provide insight worth its weight in gold. Discover what you need to know to truly experience the most rewarding years of your life, how passions perhaps long forgotten can be rediscovered, and how to achieve and maintain vibrant, good health. If you are near or in retirement, this book is a must read.*

Logan Franklin
Author, *Living a Fitness Lifestyle* and *Gray Iron: A Fitness Guide for Senior Men and Women*
www.Senior-Exercise-Central.com

If you desire a satisfying retirement, you need this book. The authors have provided a road map, with very practical advice, for a rewarding and productive time of retirement; but, like a long term corporate strategy, success requires advanced planning. Their insights are remarkably pertinent and prescient. They point out, for example, that in this stage of your life, you need to create the daily habits that build and sustain your energy level; critical to your well-being.

Dr. Alan Halpern
Orthopedic Surgeon
Author, *Runner's World Knee Book*

In Your Retirement Quest, *Spector and Lawrence have given retirees and those approaching retirement practical tips, plans, and tools to "live life fully." Useful worksheets and self-reflection tools outline plans to maintain fitness, energy, and well-being. How to maintain, develop, and build a vibrant network of friends, family, and community, the hallmark of successful "connectedness," is also highlighted. A must read for anyone approaching this phase of life! I will highly recommend this book to all my coaching clients!*

Cindy Charlton
Licensed Psychologist, Executive Coach, Communications Specialist

Alan Spector and Keith Lawrence fill a huge void for Baby Boomers. When I hosted a LifeScape seminar at our church, I saw firsthand that many people do very little retirement planning. LifeScape and Your Retirement Quest *wisely detail the importance of thinking through your personal growth, values, connectedness, mission, passion, and serving others to prepare for the well-rounded and truly fulfilling retirement we all desire. I highly recommend the valuable principles and practical approach of* Your Retirement Quest.

Jim Toy
Community Pastor, Vineyard Community Church, Cincinnati, Ohio

Your Retirement Quest

10 Secrets
for Creating and Living
a Fulfilling Retirement

Alan Spector and Keith Lawrence

Your Retirement Quest
10 Secrets For Creating And Living A Fulfilling Retirement

by Alan Spector and Keith Lawrence

Cover and text design: Brent Beck, www.brentbeck.com
Published by Cincinnati Book Publishers, www.cincybooks.com
Anthony W. Brunsman, President

ISBN – 13   978-0-9817269-8-4
ISBN – 10   0-9817269-8-4

Printed by John S. Swift Co., Inc
Printed in the United States of America
First Edition, 2010
Second Printing, 2013
Third Printing, 2016
Fourth Printing, 2018

Dedications

To Alan's Boston grandchildren, Jacob and Zoe Spector; St. Louis grandchildren, Jordan and Aaron DeBlasi; and Ann, his wife of over four decades and retirement partner; all who help Alan live a fulfilling retirement

Ann Spector

Sue Lawrence

To Keith's wife, Sue, who makes every day of retirement a blessing; his late father, Howard Lawrence, who role-modeled a fulfilling retirement; his mother, Patricia Lawrence, whose unwavering faith and support have enabled Keith to reach this exciting juncture in his life; and his loving children, Jared, Jenny, Kristal, Lauren, and Michelle

Nancy Riesz

Bob Miller

To Nancy Riesz and Bob Miller, our LifeScape, LLC partners, who have taught us so much about retirement, teamwork, friendship, and living fully

Acknowledgments

Nancy Riesz and Bob Miller—you are our friends and LifeScape partners; now you are collaborators for our book. Thank you.

We are honored that Dave Ulrich, Doug Matthews, and Tony Schwartz took time out of your demanding schedules to provide insight and support to our effort by crafting Forewords for the book.

Thank you, Peter Schiff, who persisted in his editing of the book, even as your back surgery approached. May your recovery be swift and complete.

Thank you to Dan Kiley for sharing your experience and mastery in the development of the "Financial Security" chapter.

Thank you to Tony Brunsman and Brent Beck, who, again, provided publishing and graphic design expertise, insight, and support.

To all of those who allowed us to tell your stories, thereby helping others learn from your experiences, thank you.

To the many who took the time to review the book and provide endorsements, thank you for your support.

Thank you to Hilary Sachar—you applied your precious time and extensive talents to developing www.YourRetirementQuest.com.

Many people have helped us along our journey, both in our lives and in the creation of this book. We thank you for your support, your insights, and your friendships. Thank you to Barry Macy, Joe Demarco, Ron Steele, Dave Hanna, Sonny Jandial, John Lame, Tom Regan, Mike Krug, Paul Butler, Stu Winby, Bill Goodwin, Ron and Carol White, Dick Burns, Jon Delong, Gayle Nesselhuf, Terry and Susan Galvin, Barbara Czestochowa, Deborah Schroeder-Saulnier, Tim Arnold, Mike Fleischmann, Jill Chapin, Joanna Baymiller, and the multitude of Alan's high school classmates who have helped.

Thank you especially to our wives, Sue Lawrence and Ann Spector, for giving us the love, patience, and support to pursue our passions and make this book and our fulfilling retirements possible.

Table of Contents

Introduction

"This is my quest, to follow that star..."
Don Quixote (Man of La Mancha)

"Secrets are made to be found out with time."
Charles Sanford

Through the phases of your life, whether you are young and growing up, building a career, or building a family, your future has been filled with both great promise and great uncertainty. During each life phase, you knew you had a lot to learn—and learn you did. You learned from parents and teachers, bosses and mentors, and family and friends. You studied at school, were trained and coached at work, and read about parenting at home. You observed the world around you and emulated your peers, your co-workers, and other families.

In each life phase, you were on a quest for knowledge, personal growth, and fulfillment, and you came to recognize that you did not need to blaze your own trail. Rather, you could learn from those who had gone before, just as they had learned from others. While your life is unique, you also share life's journey with others. You are on your personal quest, yet have the opportunity to acquire and use the secrets of success others have learned along the way.

The next phase of your life is no different in that *Your Retirement Quest* will be more successful when you learn and apply secrets from others. Retirement is also similar to other phases of your life in that it, too, is filled with both great promise and great uncertainty.

Prospective retirees use words like "anticipation," "freedom," and "elation" when referring to their feelings about their upcoming big day. They also use words like "anxiety," "uncertainty," "stress," and even "fear." Part of our intent in writing this book is to help you bring more certainty to your retirement future. We also hope to help free you from the negative emotions that drain your energy, affect your productivity at work and joy at home, and diminish your excitement about this major life transition.

Although there are many similarities between retirement and the other phases of your life, there is also an important difference—in retirement, it is not as obvious from whom you will be learning. Who knows the secrets?

In your youth, you lived at home and your parents were there, and you went to school and your teachers were there. During your career, you went to work and your boss and more experienced colleagues were there. As you built your family, your parents were available, as were others, like the pediatrician. When it is time for retirement, who is there for you? There are a multitude of resources, but you need to seek them out—they do not just show up.

At a time when your life journey becomes a retirement quest, having access to the learning of those who have gone before you is exactly what you need. You want to and need to know the secrets and have a roadmap for your quest.

It is, therefore, our further intent to help you on *Your Retirement Quest* and to share the *10 Secrets for Creating and Living a Fulfilling Retirement*.

There is another reason we wrote the book. Anxiety about the future is far from uncommon, especially among the most experienced workforce, those employees within sight of retirement. This cohort of employees, who are between 55 and 64 years old, is the fastest growing segment in the last decade in the United States, Europe, and Japan.

Unfortunately, uncertainty about their future is at the foundation of the trend toward these most experienced employees being increasingly distracted and disengaged at work. This trend is good for neither the employees nor their employers. Disengaged employees who stay with their companies are less productive and have higher absentee rates. Those who retire (Boomers are retiring at a rate of about 10,000 per day across the U.S.) take with them important institutional knowledge and memory.

Our contention is that one key to reengaging the experienced employee is to create more clarity of vision and a plan for his or her future; years which have the promise of being the best years of his or her life. This book, based on the proven, practical approach of LifeScape Solutions™, enables individuals to gain greater insight and confidence through the development of their personal and holistic plan—helping them in quest of a meaningful future. The book also enables employers to rejuvenate the engagement of these extraordinary employees. Our intent is that both the employee and the employer will benefit.

In summer 2009, Nancy Riesz and Bob Miller partnered with us to create LifeScape, LLC, a program to help future and current retirees plan for and experience the most fulfilling retirement they can. We collectively read hundreds of retirement books and web sites and reviewed the relevant research. We also interviewed experienced retirees, many whose stories you will read in this book, learning from well over 200 years of their cumulative retirement experiences.

Based on our research, interviews, and personal experiences, we developed the LifeScape Solutions™ model for a fulfilling retirement as well as a practical approach by which you can develop, implement, and renew your unique plan. We also discovered the *10 Secrets for Creating and Living a Fulfilling Retirement* that complement the model. Importantly, while we recognize the need for financial security and have included it in the model, our approach focuses on the too-often neglected non-financial aspects of retirement.

You can learn more about LifeScape Solutions™ at:
www.YourRetirementQuest.com

Any quest has three segments. It is critical to first envision where you are going. Once you formulate your vision, you must figure out how you are going to proceed—to establish your plan so you can embrace the journey. Finally, as your vision comes into view, it is time to enjoy the rewards.

Because you are on a quest in search of a fulfilling retirement, we have structured the book (see the Appendix, "How to Use This Book") to reflect the three segments:

Envision Your Quest

Embrace The Journey

Enjoy The Rewards

The book is also structured to reveal the *10 Secrets for Creating and Living a Fulfilling Retirement*. There is a full listing on pages 13 and 14, and you will also find the secrets highlighted where they are most relevant. Look for this icon.

Envision Your Quest—Chapters 1 through 6 will provide you with a foundation upon which to envision the possibilities of your fulfilling retirement. You will learn how our generation's definition of retirement differs from that of preceding generations and, importantly, why the new definition is critical to how you can and must think about your future. You will learn about the stages you can expect to go through as you journey through retirement, and you will be exposed to the key elements that will make up your personal plan. Every quest requires a challenge, and we will issue one for your consideration before you get started.

Embrace The Journey—Chapters 7 through 17 will enable you to establish the unique personal plan that is right for you—a plan that you can embrace. We will describe the practical planning approach in detail; walk you through each key element to consider for your plan; help you think about your critical choices and how to collaborate with those closest to you; and then guide you in putting your plan together.

Enjoy The Rewards—Whether in business or personal life, "The best-laid schemes of mice and men go often askew." Research and our experience indicate that this occurs for two reasons. First, regardless of a plan's quality, if you do not have a good approach to actually do what you have chosen to do, the plan is virtually useless. Second, if you do not renew your plan when new opportunities present themselves or life circumstances change, which they inevitably do, your plan will grow stale as will you. Chapters 18 through 20 will help you avoid these pitfalls, help you better envision how to live fully, and send you on your way to enjoy your future.

We recommend you begin *Your Retirement Quest* as early as five years before the "big day." However, we also know there are those of you whose retirements occur before you are fully ready (e.g., corporate downsizing, change in life circumstances), and we know there are those of you already retired who are not getting as much out of your life as you would hope. If you are in either of these circumstances, the book is designed for you as well.

Retirees who are currently enjoying retirement will also benefit from this book. Why? You may be seeking even more from your retirement, taking it to the "next level." Also, regardless of your current level of satisfaction, there will be changes in your life situation over time that can and will cause you to reassess your retirement activities and refresh what you are doing. You will learn a practical approach to best deal with these inevitably changing circumstances.

Our book, therefore, is for you—whether you are planning to retire, newly retired, long retired, or wishing you had never retired. We are confident that when you complete this book, you will be well along *Your Retirement Quest* toward a fulfilling retirement. Envision your future, embrace the journey and enjoy the rewards.

Alan Spector and Keith Lawrence

Forewords

Authors' note: When we considered whom to approach to write a Foreword for our book, we sought the thought-leaders in fields critical to living a fulfilling retirement: well-being and personal energy, life transition planning, and building on personal strengths. We are pleased to be able to share multiple Forewords with you, written by prominent people in their respective fields.

Dave Ulrich is a Professor of Business at the Ross School of Business at the University of Michigan, has authored 15 books covering topics in Human Resources and Leadership, has been ranked the #1 Management Educator and Guru by *BusinessWeek*, was named the most influential person in Human Resources by HR Magazine for three years, and has been on the World's Top 50 Business Thinkers since 2007.

Doug Matthews is the President and Chief Operating Officer of Right Management, a global leader in employment services. During his career, Doug was the Executive Vice President for Right Management Career Transition Services.

Tony Schwartz is President, Founder, and Chief Executive Officer of The Energy Project and a best-selling author. He is a long-time writer and journalist, as well as a consultant for *Fortune 500* companies. His newest book is *The Way We're Working Isn't Working: The Four Forgotten Needs That Energize Great Performance.*

Retire Retirement

I am generally not affected by my birthdays or the prospect of aging. But, when I hit 55 a few years ago, something felt off-kilter. After a few weeks, I realized that this was the age at which my father retired. He left over 30 years of government service to pursue other passions. He and my mom traveled and spent time with grandchildren, and he spent two to three hours a day five days most weeks distributing surplus or day-old food from grocery stores to homeless shelters and food kitchens. His retirement years were meaningful to him because he filled them with good works. I struggled to decide if my professional work was providing me with meaning in similar ways or if I should "retire" and shift more time to family and volunteer work.   While I have chosen to continue professional works, my father taught me by example that we need to redefine retirement.

This excellent guidebook by Alan Spector and Keith Lawrence offers insights, assessments, and cases of how to prepare for and deal with inevitable retirement. The authors present some startling statistics that capture the scope of retirement challenges:

- 10,000 people a day will retire!
- Most people spend less time planning for retirement than for a two week vacation.
- The average retiree spends 43 hours each week watching TV.
- Retiring is as stressful as getting married, losing your job, or having a close family member become ill.
- The highest suicide rate in the US for any segment of the population is men over 70; 50% higher than the suicide rate for teenagers.
- Only 35% of retirees have a written plan for their future finances.
- The average person today has 1.5 friends compared to three a decade ago.
- Only 27% of retirees do community service.
- Less than 4% of retirees invest more than 4 hours per week helping others.

These data suggest that we need to rethink our models and approaches to retirement (Tammy Erickson claimed the clever phrase, "retire retirement").

While many leaders are focusing on Generation Y employees, we need to remember that the "bonus year" employees (those employees who may retire at 60 and live into their 80s) have enormous experience and years of productivity ahead of them. Wise companies will find ways to continue to engage this workforce. Mature employees may continue to contribute to their organizations by mentoring others, by working part time, and by bringing lessons of history to bear on the problems of tomorrow.

But, for those who choose to retire, the message is clear: find meaning. In the last few years, Wendy Ulrich (wife and psychologist) and I, who are confessed meaning junkies, have culled many disciplines to identify how people create meaning. Meaning is generally not randomly discovered by wandering around; it is intentionally created and fashioned by explicit and thoughtful actions.

Simply stated, retirees who create meaning will have more abundant lives than those who do not. Hundreds of people showed up at my father's funeral, because they had a meaningful experience with my dad, and he with them. He knew the life challenges of the manager of the local produce department in the grocery store; he cared for those in need; he wrote thousands of letters of support to those he met; he gave flowers to the bank tellers. He created a meaningful life.

In our work to discover the "why" of work, we found seven factors that shape a meaningful experience. These seven factors overlay perfectly with the 10 secrets Spector and Lawrence reveal and the fulfilling retirement model they propose. As people prepare for retirement, they need to answer seven questions (see *The Why of Work):*

- **Identity:** Who am I? What are the strengths I bring to my bonus years and how can I use those strengths to strengthen others? (Secret #6 Mindset)
- **Purpose:** Where am I going? What motivates me and how do I spend my "free" time doing things that are consistent with my personal purpose? (Secret #3 Quest; Secret #5 Holistic)
- **Relationships:** Who do I travel with? Who are the friends I will connect with who will bring joy and meaning to my life in my family and social network? (Secret #7 Team Effort)

- **Environment:** How do I organize my retirement setting? What values will I bring into my retirement lifestyle? How will I build my physical setting to complement my emotional desires? (Secret #4 Planning)
- **Challenge:** What challenges will I continue to work on that are easy, energizing, and enjoyable to me? (Secret #1 Freedom; Secret #10 Time)
- **Learning and resilience:** How will I continue to grow and learn and recover from the inevitable mistakes along the way? (Secret #8 Action; Secret #9 Resilience)
- **Delight:** Where will I find fun and joy along my bonus year journey? (Secret #2 More Than Money)

These questions are as relevant for Gen Y as they are for the bonus year retirees. This retirement guidebook is a fantastic roadmap for answering these questions so that those who retire will continue to find meaning that creates abundance. The ideas in *Your Retirement Quest* are simple, but magical; the cases are compelling and personal; the exercises are insightful and useful.

This is a great book. Some, like my father, stumble into retirement and are able to create the meaning they seek. Others need roadmaps to lead us into this journey so that we can make the bonus years a windfall of opportunity and meaning. When I do choose to shift from my present full time professional interests to pursue other activities, I hope that I can keep in mind the clear counsel in this excellent guidebook.

Dave Ulrich
Professor, Ross School of Business, University of Michigan
Partner, The RBL Group (www.rbl.net)

Planning Your Second Life

In my career at Right Management, I have had the opportunity to work directly and indirectly with thousands of our client companies' employees who have been dealing with major career and life transitions. I have found no more challenging situation than that of a company's most experienced employees moving toward the end of their careers and through their transition into retirement.

It is in that regard that *Your Retirement Quest* stands as the valuable and authoritative resource; assisting people who are wrestling with retirement decisions on every front of their lives. We tend to think of retirement decisions only as financial in nature when in fact, as *Your Retirement Quest* so comprehensively outlines, there are actually 10 secrets for creating and living a fulfilling retirement, with finances being only one aspect.

The career and life transition ahead of the most experienced employees affects employers as well. Forty percent or more of the current workforce are contemplating retirement but would be willing to work on a more flexible basis – yet employers, in general, are not proactively engaging this vital talent even as skill shortages will soon become a reality.

The one constant I have found to be most helpful in any transition, especially the significant move into retirement, is the value of planning. This is true for both the employee and the employer. This book, therefore, is for everyone. The practical approach provides a simple yet holistic way to define our own individual "second lives;" helping ensure that each person can define a purpose and plan for his or her life, particularly as he or she moves closer to the major life transition that is retirement. This process promises new beginnings; don't leave home without it!

Doug Matthews
President and Chief Operating Officer of Right Management

Retiring Smart

We boomers never really believed we'd get older – much less *old* – but the evidence is increasingly undeniable. Ten thousand of us are *retiring* every day. However much we may have looked forward to a time in life when we didn't have to get up and commute to the office every morning, precious few of us have spent much time thinking about what to do with ourselves when that day finally arrives.

No wonder one-third of all men over 65 years old end up depressed within a year of retiring. Work has been the primary source of meaning and the biggest occupier of daytime hours for many men and women now retiring. Filling those hours doesn't happen automatically. As Janis Joplin, the consummate boomer-who-never-grew-up, once put it, "Freedom's just another word for nothing left to lose."

I've spent most of my adult life reading, thinking, writing and speaking about what it takes to live a productive, satisfying life, on and off the job. A raft of data now supports the view that in order to thrive, we need to systematically build and renew four separate sources of energy: physical, emotional, mental, and spiritual.

This is true no matter what our age, and it's especially so as we get older and can no longer take it for granted that we'll have the energy we need to live the life we want. Maintaining a full reservoir of energy across each of the four key dimensions requires a high level of intentionality. In purely practical terms, that requires building highly specific rituals into your life to assure that you translate your intentions around your retirement into behaviors and practices that stick.

Keith Lawrence and Alan Spector are both retired, but only in the most technical sense of the word. Both of them work out regularly, volunteer in several nonprofits, travel widely, and are deeply involved with their families. Somehow, they've also found time to write the book you're now holding, *Your Retirement Quest*, which provides a rich roadmap to assuring that during these years, you're not only financially secure, but also healthy, happy, intellectually challenged, and focused on what matters most to you.

Most thinking people do about retirement is around financial planning, and most of us don't even do that very well. Lawrence and Spector start there, but then cast a much wider net. In this book, they'll take you through the five predictable stages of what they call "the retirement journey" and then define the ten key elements to assure that this stage of your life is rich and satisfying.

The ground of a successful retirement is your physical well-being. Most of us pay far too little attention to our health throughout our lives. As Lawrence and Spector point out, ninety per cent of Americans get less than 30 minutes of exercise per day. As we age, we truly begin to pay the price. Your energy is your most precious resource. Taking care of your body becomes critical not just as a protection against heart disease, diabetes and other illnesses, but also as a means to assuring that you can do everything you want to do.

This book is a roadmap to the path ahead. Awareness is always the first step, and *Your Retirement Quest* first lays out what you can expect at each juncture. The key is to develop a plan that encompasses all dimensions of your life before you actually retire. If you are already retired, then this is an opportunity to consider putting more intentional structure into your days.

Regardless of where you are in this process today, this book will help you design a more fulfilling path for all the tomorrows ahead.

Tony Schwartz

Founder and CEO of The Energy Project

Author of four *New York Times* bestsellers

(most recent: *The Way We're Working Isn't Working: The Four Forgotten Needs that Energize Great Performance*)

The 10 Secrets

Our research and, especially, our interviews with retirees, many whose stories you will read in the book, have revealed *10 Secrets for Creating and Living a Fulfilling Retirement.* We have placed the secrets in the book where they are most directly addressed, although you will find insights about the secrets throughout the book, including in the personal stories. The secrets will be denoted by this icon.

Secret 1: Freedom
- Retirement sets you truly free for the first time in your life.
- Take advantage of freedom from work obligations and stress, freedom of choice and action, and freedom to explore, discover, and pursue your passions.

Secret 2: More Than Money
- Retirement is about much more than the money.
- The best things in life are not the things; plan your financial security, then focus on what really counts to you.

Secret 3: Quest
- Retirement is a journey with five distinct stages; and some people get stuck.
- Understand them, know which stage you are in, and know how to move forward.

Secret 4: Planning
- Retirement is exciting, but also unnerving, causing some to hesitate to think about and plan for their future.
- Create a holistic plan before you retire to reduce the anxiety and increase the odds of a fulfilling retirement.

Secret 5: Holistic
- There are 10 critical areas that make up a fulfilling retirement; many of them are overlooked.
- You will live fully when you embrace each of the key elements in your life.

Secret 6: Mindset
- Retirement is a state of mind—if you think you are old, you will be.
- Have a positive mindset and think and act as if you did not know how old you are—it will permeate every other aspect of your retirement.

Secret 7: Team Effort
- Your retirement affects those closest to you and making lasting change to get the most out of retirement requires their input and support.
- Identify, recruit, and involve your team; those who will help you on your quest.

Secret 8: Action
- Retirement begins now; you never know what tomorrow may bring.
- Don't wait to act on what is important to you—act now, even if you have yet to retire –"practice retirement."

Secret 9: Resiliency
- Retirement life is always evolving, sometimes in positive ways, sometimes not.
- Be resilient—be open to new opportunities, be receptive to change, and accept the reality of and adapt to setbacks.

Secret 10: Time
- Time is the most precious resource you have—you can never get it back
- Apply the LifeScape Solutions™ approach to make the best use of your time in the best years of your life.

Envision Your Quest

Envision a time in your life when you have the freedom to choose what to do, when to do it, and who you want to do it with. It is a time in your life when you are full of energy and contented at the same time. Your life is full of close relationships with family and friends; you are contributing your time and resources to helping others; your days, weeks, months, and years are filled with activities that you love, that help you grow, and that are just plain fun. You awaken each day with a positive attitude about life and are clear about your life's purpose and your personal values. You have the resources and general well-being to live the life that makes you happy and can foresee living it well into your future. You take advantage of new-found opportunities and you deal well with life's inevitable setbacks, because you are resilient and have a plan that helps guide you through them.

That time in your life can and should be in front of you. Whether you are looking forward to retirement or have already retired, your future can and should be full and fulfilling—it is well worth the quest.

We will frequently refer to living a full and fulfilling life in retirement. But what does that mean? The answer will be different for each individual, but you will know it when you see it. You will also know when you are not living that way. Here is what some retirees said when asked to describe what a fulfilling retirement means to them.

- "Doing what I want, with whom I want, when I want, and if I want"
- "Having the clarity and energy to pursue a life of meaning and happiness

for me and others"

- "Being satisfied, being comfortable, and doing the things I most want to do"
- "Living life so when I die, I have no regrets"
- "Awakening with joy each morning, falling asleep contented, and living with gratitude"
- "Being busy with and challenged by things I choose to do and having fun doing them"
- "Exercising the freedom I have earned to live the life I choose"
- "Living my life with purpose"
- "Going to sleep at night knowing I had a full day making a difference to someone—myself, family, friends, strangers"

You may already have a vision of what you want your future to be, or you may not. Regardless, as you proceed through the book, your vision will come into focus, and, importantly, you will be taking the steps to move toward that vision.

This first section of the book will focus on helping you envision *Your Retirement Quest* before moving onto later sections that will help you develop and implement your plan. In this book section, you will learn why "Retirement Is the Wrong Word," but why we will continue to use it anyway.

"Freedom" can be a meaningful part of your retirement vision. You will experience the freedom from many of the things that drained you while you were working; the freedom of choice and action; and the freedom to pursue your passions.

Financial security is an essential element in building a robust retirement plan, and, frequently, the only thing many prospective and current retirees focus on. Financial security is important, but you will learn in this section why "It's Not All about the Money" when planning for a fulfilling retirement.

Virtually everyone goes through five "Stages of Retirement," beginning when we are still many years away from the big day. Understanding these stages will help you envision your future and to deal with each stage as it arises.

Finally, in this section, we will begin the discussion about "Planning Retirement." In doing so, we will share a real-life example of a planned and fulfilling retirement, then share an approach that will help you think about your own planning.

Before you begin to Envision Your Quest, however, there is a reality to consider—change and planning are difficult and can be unsuccessful. Our first chapter, therefore, is intended to share that reality with you in a way we hope will help you "Get Serious about Your Retirement."

Chapter 1

Get Serious about Your Retirement

*"Change is the law of life, and those who look only
to the past or present are certain to miss the future."*
John F. Kennedy

"I'll go anywhere as long as it's forward."
David Livingstone

The Challenge

Understand what it takes to make a change in your life and beat the odds, so that you will be able to create a better retirement life for yourself.

The Rationale

Every good quest needs a challenge. Don Quixote's challenge was to "dream the impossible dream." Our challenge to you is to "dream the possible dream."

Making meaningful, lasting change in your life is difficult. There are many reasons for this, but despite the reasons and the difficulty, you can be successful.

It is not our objective in this chapter to be pessimistic or alarmist. Rather, we are being realistic and hope you will be also. If you are, you will be more likely to take the necessary steps to make the changes that will best move you toward living fully and experiencing a fulfilling retirement.

We assume, because you are reading this book, that you are interested in changing. You may still be working in your primary career and anticipating the transition to retirement with both excitement and trepidation. You know change is coming and want to manage it so it does not manage you.

You may already be retired and reading this book because you believe you could and should be living a fuller and more meaningful retirement life. If that is true for you, we can infer that you want change as well and want to manage the change to ensure a satisfying result.

Some retirees have told us that when they were working and focused on their careers, they ignored or were insensitive to non-work-related issues in their lives; for example, family or health problems. When they retired, there was no longer a buffer or a distraction—the issues were front and center. They have had to face them and make changes if they expected to resolve the issues. You may be among this group.

It is also possible that you are not looking to change your life, because you are already happy. If that is the case, you may be reading this book to help validate what you are doing, and we applaud you for that. We suggest, however, that you will likely be dealing with change in the future, because evolving life circumstances will inevitably cause you to do so. In that regard, our challenge is for you as well.

We are sensitive to the reality that you may have complicating circumstances in your life. These special considerations may be adding anxiety, complexity, and instability, making it even more difficult to make the changes you want and need—perhaps when those changes would be most helpful.

Examples of special considerations are dealing with aging parents, dealing with your own aging and how our culture views it, losing a friend or loved one, being a single parent, living alone, spending more time than you planned caring for your grandchildren, addressing a personal illness, supporting "boomerang" children, living through a divorce, or perhaps just dealing with the changes in your life that derive from knowing retirement is coming.

Whether you are dealing with special considerations or simply trying to enhance your life, this book will be helping you identify those changes that will impact you the most. Change is difficult and requires a commitment, but you can do it, we can help, and the results are worth the effort.

Despite the fact that the United States is the wealthiest nation on the planet, we rank 15th in the world in our level of happiness. Denmark, Ireland, Switzerland, Canada, Puerto Rico, and others rank ahead of us. The data indicate that many Americans are dissatisfied with their lives for any number of reasons. They may, for example, be bored, feel lonely, not like their physical appearance or level of fitness, or be financially insecure. One would think Americans' unhappiness would provide a huge source of motivation to "change" to make things better.

Unfortunately, most people, even those with good reason to do so, are not successful making a meaningful change in their lives. For example, someone who knows he or she needs to lose weight to be healthier may make a New Year's resolution to take off the pounds. Yet, on average, he or she will make the same resolution ten times before beginning to act on it and less than 10% will succeed in taking the pounds off and keeping them off.

This difficulty of making changes is not unique to individuals. It is also true for companies and organizations. Making change on any scale is very hard work, and, in most cases, attempts to do so fail. For example, 75% of acquisitions in industry do not meet their objectives. Sixty percent of new restaurants go under in the first three years. Numerous attempts to improve the efficiency of governmental organizations have yielded little success. Why is this?

There are many reasons why changing is a daunting task. In the book, *Influencer: The Power To Change Anything*, Kerry Patterson and co-authors speak of the need to "pull all the levers" to overcome the many barriers to change. We have distilled the "levers" down to three key factors—"skill, will, and support."

Skill—do you have the knowledge to act differently? Said another way, if someone provided you with clear motivation, like telling you they would give you a million dollars to make a change, would you even know what to do and how to do it? We will suggest that you take steps to develop the skills you need, enjoy the learning process, and practice the activities that will make your life more meaningful.

Will—are you really committed to doing something different in your life? You can measure this by answering this two-part question, "Am I ready to take the first step in the next 24 hours and focus on sustaining the change over the next 21 days?" If you do not act virtually immediately and if you do not keep going for a reasonable period of time, the chances of you doing anything longer term are almost zero. We will suggest that you identify and take initial steps in each of the key activities of your retirement plan. We will also provide you with the compelling reasons for you to consider making a change in the key elements of your life. In many ways, the gist of this book is to give you the knowledge you need to have the will to build your unique plan and then make that plan happen.

Support—skill and will focus on you, while support is focused on your environment. There are two factors in this regard. First, is there someone who will partner with you to support you in your change? For example, if you want to begin an exercise program, is there someone who will go to the gym or take daily walks with you? Having a partner serves to help you hold yourself accountable for making the change and sticking to it. The second factor is your surroundings—does your environment support your new way of living? For example, do you have the right food in the house to support your desire to change your eating habits?

A great example of how difficult it is to change and how support is critical has to do with the shocking statistics about those recovering from heart attacks. Despite just having gone through a life-threatening event, only 20% of heart-attack victims make meaningful long-term behavioral changes. What do those who do make a change have in common? They have someone in their life who is there for them—to encourage them, hold them accountable, and truly care about their well-being. We will be asking you to identify the person in your life who can best help you with support. You will find that this may be different people for the different changes you choose to make.

The answer, therefore, to why change is so difficult is that we either do not recognize the need for skill, will, and support, or we are aware, but do not develop them when making a change. All three must be in place to make and sustain change over time.

The good news about planning your retirement is two-fold. First, you will find that many of the things you are already doing to make your life meaningful require only that you continue them. For these areas, change will not be necessary. Second, we are confident, based on our personal experience and the experiences of those whose stories you will read, that you can meet the challenge we have laid out for you. Although doing so is not a cake walk, it can be done, and the benefits are well worth the dedication to the task. Be one of those who works through the entire book; makes your best effort to build your plan; and creates the skill, will, and support to make change in your life.

A fulfilling retirement awaits.

Chapter 2

Retirement is the Wrong Word

"Retirement is the ugliest word in the language."
Ernest Hemmingway

"There is a whole new kind of life ahead, full of experiences just waiting to happen. Some call it 'retirement.' I call it bliss."
Betty Sullivan

Do You Know?

The late American clergyman, Harry Emerson Fosdick, said, "Don't simply retire from something; have something to retire to."

There is no word for "retirement" in Okinawa—they have a related word that translates to "purpose."

Why "Retirement is the Wrong Word"

When you search a dictionary and thesaurus for the word "retirement," you find negative connotations. Synonyms are "departure," "leaving," "withdrawal," and "retreat." One definition reads, "a state of being withdrawn from the rest of the world or from a former busy life." These give retirement a sense of ending rather than beginning.

Yet, retiring from your primary work career is not merely an act of ending, but, more opportunistically, an act of beginning and of the promise of a positive future. We sought to find a word to better reflect the optimism of this next phase of life. Keith Lawrence, for example, uses the word, "graduation." There were many words and phrases we considered and others have used, but, in the end, we decided to use "retirement" anyway. Why? The word is well established in our lexicon, and it serves well to describe a "time" in our lives, albeit not the "condition" of our lives.

You will find, therefore, "retirement" used despite it being the wrong word. Throughout the book, both you and we must keep in mind the word's limitations. The intent of this chapter is to help you envision the future such that when you read the word "retirement," you think not of "withdrawal," but of "opportunity;" not of "departure," but of "fulfillment;" not of "retreat," but of "engagement."

Worn-Out Treads

Perhaps there is a different way to think about the word "retirement." Think of yourself as a finely tuned automobile. You have traveled the road of life, rumbled over speed bumps, accelerated on straight-aways, strained up steep hills, struggled to maintain control on winding curves, confronted dead ends, obeyed stop signs, navigated U-turns, and suffered the occasional fender bender.

As you approach the end of your primary work career, you realize your chassis is still in pretty good shape, although it may need some bodywork and fresh paint. Although it may have lost some horsepower, your engine is still operating well. This bodes well for the future, because you are excited about continuing your travels.

You do notice, however, that your tires are worn—the treads are bare and traction is hard to come by. You come to the conclusion that with your solid chassis and purring engine, all you need to do to ensure safe and exciting travel are two things.

First, install a GPS to help you know how to get where you are going—which roads to take, where to turn, and when it is time to recalculate your path as you embark on the next leg of your life journey.

Second, you need to replace those worn-out treads. You do not want to lose traction. It is time to "re-tire."

Retirement-Busy is Good

What retirement will be and can be is changing, because demographics are changing. The concept of retirement was declared in the latter half of the 19th century by the Prussian/German statesman Chancellor Otto Von Bismarck. Bismarck was besieged politically and needed to regain popular support. To relieve the political pressure, he declared that the government would pay a pension to any non-working German over the age of 65. His policy did two things. First, it set the arbitrary world standard for retirement age. Secondly, it assured the German government would pay few pensions—less than one percent of Germans lived to be 65 at the time.

Life expectancy has been growing ever since. In the United States, about the time of Bismarck's social program, the average life expectancy was only 42 years for white males (to choose a standard group for this comparison). By 1935, when Social Security was enacted, the life expectancy average had risen to 60. When AARP was founded in 1958, average life expectancy was approaching 68, and today has grown to 78.

The average longevity of those who live long enough to retire is even higher. Someone living to 60 can now expect to live into his or her early-80s; those living to 70 can expect to reach the mid-80s; and those living to 80 can expect to reach the upper-80s. The numbers are even higher for white females, who live an average of seven years longer than their male counterparts in the United States.

The steep rise in life expectancy in only the last 50 years has changed the nature of retirement. In the Bismarck era, one could not expect to retire. Now, on average, we can expect to live 20 to 30 years or more in retirement. One way to think about this is that when you retire, you have 1000 to 1500 or more weeks to make the most of—the new demographics are an opportunity for a new perspective on what your retirement life should and could be.

The old view of retirement, assuming one lived that long, was that it was an ending, a winding down, the final years, a passive lifestyle, reliance on others, no need to plan, pure leisure the goal, no schedules to keep. This view was driven by the fact that people were retiring in their "old age," having worked hard and more frequently at manual labor, with relatively little time remaining.

The new view is based on longer retirement expectations. We are now retiring at a "young age," having, in general, worked less physically hard than previous generations, with much more time remaining in our lives. The opportunity presented by this new view is that we have time in retirement to renew old passions and find new ones, live a balanced and enriching life, be actively engaged, have the freedom to explore, keep busy in new and energizing ways, and do meaningful things for others.

One way to think about your possible future is to contrast being busy during your working life and being busy in your retirement—retirement-busy is good.

Work-Busy	Retirement-Busy
Mostly non-discretionary	Mostly discretionary
External stress inducers	Internal stress inducers
Structure time to survive	Structure time to enjoy
Mostly responding to business	Mostly responding to passions
"I don't have any time for anything but work."	"How did I ever have time to work?"

Retirement without Borders

We have learned from our interviews and research that the concepts, principles, and secrets for creating and living a fulfilling retirement apply across geographies. In addition, Bob Miller, one of our LifeScape, LLC partners, conducted a workshop in Europe in the winter of 2010. This is what he reported.

"The day-long session, which included Swiss, Germans, Belgians, Russians, and Americans, was a big hit and verified the validity of the LifeScape model for European nationalities. Though pension arrangements vary, there was clear consensus that, as in the US, once the financial foundation is in place, the real secrets for a fulfilling retirement are in the rest of the LifeScape Solutions™ model.

"The concept of the active and engaged life of the new retirement for Baby Boomers is as alive in Europe as it is in the US. One participant stated that the old retirement in her country is defined by the term 'pensioner' and she wanted no part of that derogatory tag. Her vision of retirement was an active lifestyle of enjoying and contributing to the Arts and of personal growth through continued learning and volunteering. Another contrasted his admiration for his father as a role model for retirement; a man who was physically active and finished writing his book just before his death at 98, compared with relatives whose retirement consists mainly of watching television.

"It was great to see and hear how LifeScape provided the awareness and motivation to start charting the retirement journeys for people around the world."

Peter Collins is a prime example of why "retirement" is the wrong word, regardless of where you live. He was born on the south coast of England, near Bournemouth, worked in the UK and the

US, before moving to work in Belgium in 1998. Five years later, he retired there. Except for a short stint in Newcastle, England, where his wife, Agnieszka, was transferred by her employer, Peter and she have continued to live in Belgium, while also traveling extensively.

Peter's retirement experience has been one of engagement, personal growth, and meaning. His activities, approach, and insights indicate that the key elements of a fulfilling retirement span geographies and cultures.

Peter spent much of his first three retirement years searching for, renovating, moving into, and establishing the home that Agnieszka and he wanted to live in. Peter did much of the renovation work and gardening himself. The home was not all-consuming, however, as he also found time over a nine-month period to pursue a lifelong dream—to build an intricate wooden model ship from a kit, given to him by his sons. During this period, Peter also travelled frequently to Scotland to support his ailing mother and found time to be on the Board of Directors of a non-profit.

Before he retired, when anyone asked Peter what he was going to do in retirement, he would answer, "Paint water colors." With everything else going on in his life, however, he found this passion waned. One day he was speaking with a former colleague who was still working. The colleague asked Peter how his painting was going. When Peter responded that the only painting he had been doing was decorating the walls of his new home, the former colleague proceeded to tell Peter that he, despite still working, had become engrossed with painting water colors and even had an upcoming exhibition. Peter felt ashamed that he had yet to begin to pursue the passion that had been his declared retirement hobby. He began painting water colors instead of just the walls in his home.

Peter has also taken up golf and is determined to drive down his handicap. He likes to hike, especially enjoying Northumberland in England. Peter enjoys reading much more than he did while working, alternating between light novels and serious works on numerous subjects. He has continued to pursue two lifelong interests, choral singing and photography, having recently moved from the darkroom to digital technology.

He is also connected with a number of groups of former colleagues and friends, whom he sees regularly. One group meets every four to six weeks and has grown into somewhat of a study group. One member reported on a friend who had passed away, saying that the spouse knew nothing of the couple's financial affairs and could not even get into her husband's computer. The group learned from this experience and developed what they refer to as the "death check list." Each of them has ensured their spouses are prepared if something should happen to them. This activity prompted the group to address other useful learning opportunities. They created a checklist of the considerations for deciding where to live in retirement and as you age, and they are now jointly writing a book about retiring in Belgium. This group and others keep Peter connected, mentally stimulated, and learning from others' experiences.

Peter travels to the United States twice per year to visit his two sons and their families, including Peter's grandchildren. He and Agnieszka, who is of Polish descent, also travel frequently around Europe, relishing the diverse cultures that are only a few hours away. They often use these trips to visit vineyards—they love wine and now only buy from vineyards they have visited. Opening the bottle reminds them of their travels and of the vintners and their families. Peter and Agnieszka, who is still working, are looking into volunteering to work at a vineyard in France when she retires this coming year.

While the couple is looking forward to Agnieszka's upcoming retirement, they are somewhat anxious about how they will create their new rhythm at home, but are confident they will happily work through it.

When asked what he has learned about retirement and what he would advise others, Peter offers compelling insights.

- Be psychologically prepared to retire by thinking about and planning for it well in advance. This helps to make the transition seamless.
- Choose your own pathway. Do not allow the expectations of others be too influential in how you choose to spend your time.
- Do not be self-limiting. Peter advises to not care how old you are—try things that others your age might shy away from if you think you want to do them.
- Follow your dreams, do new things, be spontaneous.
- Do not expect to be a different person in retirement—use your strengths and recognize your weaknesses.
- Stay focused on the important stuff without being dragged into the trivia. Peter advises, "Don't do today what you can put off until tomorrow." His

point is not to neglect important things that need to be done, but rather to resist being caught up in daily routines and trivial activities that can become a rut.

Peter is living a full and fulfilling life in retirement. He views this time of his life with a positive attitude, has abundant energy, is engaged in many activities, keeps mentally stimulated, is pursuing his passions, and is having is a lot of fun doing all of this with the woman he loves.

Not Ready to Sit Yet

In 1954, the Supreme Court ruled on Brown v. Board of Education to declare state laws establishing segregated schools to be unconstitutional. Three years later, there were still states and localities that had yet to respond to the ruling—Henderson County in Kentucky was one of them. Dorothy Clancey was a second-grader living in Henderson in 1957. She was forced, along with other "Negroes" from neighboring counties, to attend a "consolidated" school that had three teachers for eight grades. Dorothy's parents, James and Marguerite Clancey, two white ministers, the NAACP, and another African American family decided their children needed and, by Supreme Court decree, deserved a better education, closer to home. They began the campaign that eventually desegregated Henderson County schools.

Dorothy and her family had some very difficult, frightening, and dangerous years, but she learned the value of doing what is right, the value of standing up for your rights, and the value of education. Her passion for education would become her career as well as her retirement focus.

In 1960, Dorothy and her family moved to St. Louis, where she went on to graduate from Soldan High School. She went to Southeast Missouri State, Howard University, and the University of Missouri-St. Louis, where she earned her Bachelor's of Science in History and Education and her Master's in Education. Dorothy felt privileged to do her student teaching at inner-city Soldan High School, her alma mater, and honored to retire from teaching at Soldan in 2007, 35 years after she had begun.

Retired, yes, but as Dorothy puts it, "I was not ready to sit yet."

She retired, took some time off, and did some substitute teaching at a school for children with special needs (e.g., spina bifida). Dorothy fervently believes "teaching is the best profession known to man," and she soon decided to return to the education field full time, albeit in a different capacity—she is the in-school suspension teacher at suburban Parkway North High School.

Students who commit a disciplinary offense short of warranting full suspension are sent to Dorothy's room to do their schoolwork in a supervised setting. Dorothy, however, treats them as her own students and works closely with them to ensure they keep up with their work. Her biggest compliment has come when numbers of students ask to be sent to her classroom when they are behind in their work, because, even though they have done nothing wrong, they greatly value the help she provides and the positive study atmosphere she creates.

So, is Dorothy retired? Yes. Is it time for her to sit? No. For her, retirement is the wrong word. She continues to engage in her passions, education and teaching. She also plays tennis, does water aerobics, hits balls at the local driving range, gardens, reads voraciously, attends cultural events, and spends as much time as she can with her five grandchildren, ages two to 15. She shares many of these activities with her husband, Marvin, and they also share a home, along with Dorothy's mother, filled with energy, laughter, and love.

Marvin Neals and Dorothy Walker-Neals

Marvin is a retired school principal, but, like Dorothy, is busy and enjoying retirement, although that is the wrong word for him as well. In addition to sharing the things they do together, Marvin also coaches high school basketball, where he has led his team to a state championship and won coach-of-the-year honors. He loves the game, follows it closely at all levels, and joins a group of friends to attend the NCAA Final Four every year. It is also not time for Marvin to sit yet.

Fun, Stimulating, Rewarding

By any measure, John Hoffman has had both a successful career and meaningful retirement. His physics degree and MBA from Notre Dame put him in good stead as he went on to a diverse career as a software engineer for the Air Force; an engineer at General Electric, where he was involved in the early designs of CT scanners; and finally holding Quality, Regulatory, and Business Leadership roles for CTI in Knoxville.

John retired in 2002, with no clear idea what we wanted to do next. He became a consultant, helping firms comply with FDA regulations, but this work did not provide him with the deep meaning he sought in retirement. Through connections he had at Notre Dame, and with the help of friends and former colleagues, John went through a "self-guided retreat" to determine what would be meaningful to him.

While it was a major departure from his previous life roles, John discovered that his real passion was to teach at the college level, thereby gaining the personal satisfaction of helping young people develop their skills and their lives.

John Hoffman

John set about the task of reinventing himself. After being turned down as "unqualified" by ten universities because he did not have his PhD, the University of Tennessee recognized what he and his career experiences had to offer. He has been at UT ever since and proclaims, "Teaching is my retirement," a statement supported by the excitement he exhibits when he is in front of his students.

One might argue that John Hoffman is not retired, because he is still working. John would argue that he is retired, because, at age 60, he moved from a career he enjoyed to an activity about which he is passionate. While he continues to teach, he is always looking for new, exciting opportunities and recently expanded his role at UT to take on responsibilities as the Assistant Department Head in the Department of Management.

John's motto is, "As long as it is fun, stimulating, and rewarding, I will keep doing it." Retirement is the wrong word for John Hoffman, just as it is the wrong word for Peter, Dorothy, and Marvin—and can be the wrong word for you as well.

Key Learning about "Retirement is the Wrong Word"

1. Retirement today is significantly different than it was for your parents. As Tammy Erickson notes, "It's time to retire retirement."

2. Your retirement may last 20 to 30 years or more, giving you the opportunity to fully engage in enjoying a long and meaningful next phase of your life.

3. The quality of your future will in large part be determined by developing a clear picture of what you want it to be. This vision provides you with direction to help identify opportunities and make choices about how you want to best spend your time.

4. Your mindset of what retirement is and can be will have a significant influence on how you live it. Your opportunity is to think about retirement as a beginning, the new definition, versus an ending, the old definition.

Getting Started

1. Think about those you know who are already retired and whether they are living the old retirement or the new retirement. What can you learn from their lifestyles and activities that might be right for you? What excites you? What screams "Not for me!"?

2. Write down what instinctively comes to mind when you think about retirement. Review what you have written and determine if this is the retirement you want for yourself. You can use the worksheet on the next page for this exercise.

(Authors' Suggestion: Before you proceed to the worksheet on the next page, read "How to Use This Book" on pages 258 to 260 in the Appendix.)

"Retirement is the Wrong Word"
Planning Worksheet

Personal Assessment: Rate the following statement from 1 to 5:
1 = This statement is far from describing my retirement outlook.
5 = This statement fully describes my retirement outlook.

"I can envision a long and fulfilling retirement."

Rating:　　1　　2　　3　　4　　5

Personal thoughts about envisioning my retirement future:

_____

_____

_____

_____

_____

_____

_____

_____

_____

_____

The one person in my life who can best help me envision my retirement future is

_____

Chapter 3

Freedom

"Freedom, in general, may be defined as the absence of obstacles to the realization of desires."
Bertrand Russell

"Man is free at the moment he wishes to be."
Voltaire

Do You Know?

Two-thirds of Americans define freedom as doing what they want and being able to make their own choices.

Holding other things like income, gender, race, religion, politics, and family status constant, those who feel free are nearly 20 percentage points more likely to say they are very happy.

What is "Freedom?"

A friend of Keith's recently retired, and on the first morning of his retirement, he sent Keith a simple, but profound, text message, "I'm a free man." What did he mean?

Mike Ferrari had experienced several very challenging months at work, so, on the surface, his text message probably meant he was free from the stress, bureaucracy, and anxiety of his workplace. There are two things, however, that make it likely that Mike will soon take full advantage of the opportunity his new-found freedom affords him. First, he had been looking forward to having the time and flexibility to pursue the many dreams he had been putting off for years and had spent time preparing to pursue them in retirement. Second, Mike had attended a LifeScape Solutions™ seminar in which he learned about the key elements of a fulfilling retirement.

When Mike gets a little time to decompress from work, he will acknowledge that his first-morning text was prophetic, and he will discover there are three "retirement freedoms":

1. Freedom from
2. Freedom of
3. Freedom to

Regardless of whether you enjoy your career situation or not, your work ties you to obligations, required tasks, daily routines, demands from bosses, colleagues, and subordinates, the stress of deadlines, and various degrees of uncertainty and anxiety about the future. At work, your schedule is not your own, and to a large extent, how you choose to use your time is nondiscretionary. Retirement offers you the "freedom from" these previous ties and allows you to regain control of your life.

Simply retiring does not in itself remove uncertainty and anxiety about the future. Retirement does, however, allow you the "freedom of" discretionary choice and action. As you gain the knowledge of what makes up a fulfilling retirement and as you develop your unique, personalized retirement plan, you will be making choices about what you want to do and acting on those choices. Doing so will bring certainty to your future, relieve unnecessary stress, and provide a renewed sense of purpose to your life.

Retirement also enables you to take advantage of the "freedom to" discover more about who you are and guide your life in that direction; try many things even if they do not work out and learn from each time that happens; identify and pursue the things you are passionate about; and eliminate things in your life that drain your energy.

These are but a few examples we have heard from retirees of the choices that retirement freedom afforded them:

- Freedom from putting makeup on or shaving every day
- Freedom to take a nap
- Freedom from using a blow dryer
- Freedom to go to the gym everyday; or to skip a day
- Freedom from ironing or going to the drycleaners
- Freedom to go to the movies in the afternoon
- Freedom of time to just stare at my flower garden
- Freedom to attend my granddaughter's school play in the morning
- Freedom from driving during rush hour
- Freedom from long unproductive meetings
- Freedom to play golf when the course is not jammed
- Freedom to have sex on Tuesday morning *(or any morning, for that matter)*
- Freedom from performance reviews; getting them or giving them

Do you still have obligations when you retire? Certainly. Will you still have a busy life? Hopefully. Will you still have some stress, be challenged, and have some uncertainty? Yes. But, with the freedoms retirement affords you, all of this will be much more manageable and energizing rather than burdensome and draining.

Keith's friend, Mike, is actively pursuing the "freedom of" and "freedom to" along with his "freedom from" to create a full and fulfilling retirement future. You have the same opportunity.

Secret 1: Freedom
- Retirement sets you truly free for the first time in your life.
- Take advantage of freedom from work obligations and stress, freedom of choice and action, and freedom to explore, discover, and pursue your passions.

Unleashed

(Keith Lawrence) I grew up in upstate New York, one of three boys in a very typical family of the 60s and 70s. My parents were hard working and valued education, two core values they passed along to my brothers and me. They also taught me the value and responsibility of freedom and gave me the personal space to make my own decisions.

I earned my engineering degree from Rensselaer Polytechnic Institute and went on to what would be a very rewarding and fulfilling 32-year career at Procter & Gamble. Despite enjoying both my education and work experiences, I realized that during neither did I have full freedom to make my own decisions. My school and company were among the best to attend and work for, respectively, but even so, each had constraints. I understood why some of these boundaries were necessary, but also felt held back to some degree. As one of the leaders I worked with said, "It feels like I can never open up the throttle, and as a result, I run on six versus eight cylinders." It was not until I graduated (my word for "retired") in 2009 that, really for the first time in my life, I felt the full freedom that I was thirsting for since childhood.

In the late 1980s, I was assigned to propose a new organization design based on finding an answer to the question, "What leads individuals, teams, and companies to perform at their very best and sustain their success over time?"

I became fascinated with the science of high performing people and organizations. The study at work became my personal and lifelong quest and passion. I set out to learn from the very best and had the opportunity to visit with several hundred companies, academia, consultants, and renowned world leaders, among them, Colin Powell, Margaret Thatcher, Tony Blair, and Bill Clinton. Each encounter added to my collection of "golden nuggets." Along my journey, I came to realize I was not just learning about peak performance in the workplace—I was learning about peak performance in life.

My exposure to and learning from the world's best taught me the importance of envisioning and planning my life, of maintaining my health and acting the age I want to be, of managing change instead of letting it manage me, of the need to connect with and give back to others. Being a husband and a father of five taught me other important life lessons, particularly the need to really listen, to be empathetic, and to be supportive and patient. I also learned about the power of resiliency—being able to adapt to life's unexpected changes. I have been blessed throughout the years with unwavering support from family and close friends that I deeply cherish. Thirty years of learning has heavily influenced how I have thought about my future and led me to want to share what I have learned with others.

As my career progressed, I increasingly felt as though there was "more to be." I felt like a butterfly confined in its cocoon waiting to be released. Part of this was driven by working in a large established company with its many rules and procedures. Another contributor to my anxiety was not having the time and freedom to pursue other dreams that were being added almost daily to my "bucket list."

Almost a decade ago, recognizing I was feeling constrained, I added another leg to my learning quest. At that time, my dear friend, Al Spector, was retiring. I picked his brain about his decision making, his vision, and his plan. I realized it was time for me to begin to envision my retirement future and plan for my life after career.

Just as I had learned from the best regarding peak performance of organizations, so I sought to learn from the best about retirement. I began interviewing retirees, who were excited to share their stories. Their experiences and the "secrets" they shared helped me discover there is no single answer, but rather a number of key ingredients to a successful next stage of life.

Sadly, over the course of my retirement discovery quest, a few close associates unexpectedly passed away, and I watched others deal with serious illnesses. I realized there are no guarantees in life—the time to get on with "living my dream" was now. My wife, Sue, had retired from teaching a few years earlier and I was anxious to spend more time enjoying life with her and my family. I began to anticipate the freedom retirement would afford me.

I was excited and comforted to find that my learning quest and my planning led to a smooth transition. The one thing I did not envision, however, was how much I would fully appreciate how wonderful life would feel. The sense of personal liberty and freedom has been beyond expectations. For the first time in decades, I was unleashed, fully in control of my time, my obligations, and my pursuits.

Sure, there were some small things that were unnerving. Would I eat lunch with Sue every day? Who would prepare lunch? How would I introduce myself? (It would no longer be, "Hi, I'm Keith Lawrence from Procter & Gamble.")

These small adjustments were easily resolved and paled compared to the overwhelming feeling of freedom. Because my plan included a host of meaningful activities, I was immediately busy doing the things I wanted to do, when I wanted to do them, with the people I wanted to do them with. Several of my retirement activities have to do with sharing what I have learned over the years with others, with regard to both achieving peak performance and preparing for retirement. I am blessed to be in a position to "teach what I practice," "practice what I teach," and hopefully, "enable dreams" (my personal life purpose) along the way.

I continue on my retirement quest—learning, appreciating, and cherishing the freedom of every day.

Brothers and Friends

Retirement afforded Marshall Faintich the freedom of time and choice to identify and pursue a passion and make a profound connection with his brother. As Marshall was growing up, his best friend and playmate was his older brother, Dave. They did everything together—that is, with one exception. When they were teenagers, Marshall did not appreciate Dave's passion for birding and the hours he spent poring over Peterson's *Field Guide to the Birds*. Dave continued to pursue what would become a lifelong passion and, in 2007, was part of the birding party at Moon Lake Park that discovered the 500th bird species in Florida, a White Wagtail. From that point forward, his birding group would refer to themselves as the Wagtails.

In 2006, after he retired, Marshall and his wife, Alice, moved to Nellysford, Virginia, in the beautiful Wintergreen Resort community, an area replete with wildlife. After seeing the number and variety of birds at his newly-erected bird feeder, a desire to try his hand at wildlife photography was awakened within Marshall. As he writes, "At that point, I did not know the difference between a nuthatch and a titmouse, but I knew someone who did—my brother Dave."

Brothers and Birders: Marshall Faintich and David Faintich

Over the next three years, Marshall took 85,000 photos of local birds, some of which he needed Dave's help to identify. Marshall gradually needed less identification help from Dave, but e-mails continued as the two brothers and friends shared their photos and their passion. In 2009, Marshall published his book, *A Photographic Guide to the Birds of Wintergreen*.

In October 2009, Marshall traveled to St. Louis for his 45th high school reunion. He proudly but sadly carried one of his books as a gift for his brother, who still lived in their hometown, knowing that his brother Dave would most likely never see the book. Dave had suffered a heart attack a week earlier, was not doing well, and died during Marshall's reunion weekend at age 65. Marshall lost a brother, a friend, and a fellow birder.

What Marshall had gained, however, because of the freedom he experienced in retirement, was a new and fulfilling passion, the opportunity to share it with others through his book, and, of prime importance, a profound closeness with his brother through Dave's final years.

Key Learning about "Freedom"

1. An integral part of retirement is the freedom from work obligations, the freedom of time and choice, and the freedom to explore and learn.
2. Having a retirement plan helps reduce uncertainty, relieve any anxiety you may have about your future, enable you to experience more freedom, and focus your energies on being at your very best.

Getting Started

1. Think about and write down (you can use the worksheet on the next page) those things in your life that are currently sources of irritation, things that drain your energy. Circle those that you have the freedom to eliminate in retirement. These can become the basis of things you choose to "Stop" in your retirement plan— we will return to the "Stop" concept later in the book.
2. Think about and write down (using the worksheet) those things you would like to do in retirement when you have the freedom of time, choice, and action. These may be big things or seemingly small things, like the examples from other retirees earlier in this chapter.

"Freedom" Planning Worksheet

Personal Assessment: Rate the following statement from 1 to 5:
1 = This statement is far from describing how I think about retirement freedom.
5 = This statement fully describes how I think about retirement freedom.

"I can envision how my retirement freedom will make an important difference in my life."

Rating: 1 2 3 4 5

Things that are currently draining my energy: (Freedom from):

_____

_____

Things I want to do in retirement when I have the Freedom of time, choice, and action:

_____

_____

_____

Other personal thoughts about freedom in retirement and what it means to me:

_____

_____

The one person in my life who can best help me take full advantage of my freedom in retirement is _____

Chapter 4

It's Not All about the Money

"I'd like to live as a poor man with lots of money."
Pablo Picasso

"The chief value of money lies in the fact that
one lives in a world
in which it is overestimated."
H. L. Mencken

Do You Know?

Only 10% of one's happiness is determined by materialistic factors (e.g., how much money you have, the size of your home). The opportunity is to focus on the non-financial factors, such as your attitudes and behaviors.

Sixty-seven percent of 100-year olds live below the poverty level; however a full 95% feel they have enough money to meet their needs and 96% feel they are better off than others of their age.

Why "It's Not All about the Money"

We recognize that the subject of retirement finances is far from trivial. Many of us look forward to or live in retirement with a heavy dose of anxiety about our finances and, therefore, our future. This is true whether we have a relatively large nest egg or a small one. No wonder—we are constantly barraged with the cultural message that accumulating more is better and the message from the financial industry that emphasizes the sole importance of money in our retirement planning. Anxiety does not derive solely from the messaging. We also know that life circumstances can negatively affect our retirement financial security; for example, significant illness, stock market fluctuations, children unexpectedly needing support, being forced to retire before our financial plan says we are ready. It is no wonder that the recent economic downturn has increased uncertainty about what we can really count on having to live on.

That being said, it is our contention that, regardless of your financial situation,

1. you deserve a full and fulfilling retirement;
2. you can create a full and fulfilling retirement that is right for you; and

3. you will continue to and should pay attention to planning for your financial security (which we will address in more detail in Chapter 10).

The February 2010 edition of *Consumer Reports* cited a survey of more than 24,000 on-line subscribers, among them a large sampling of retirees. One could look at the results and conclude that the size of one's nest egg is a major predictor of the level of satisfaction in retirement. This is because the data show a 20 percentage point increase in satisfaction as net worth went from $250,000 to $500,000. The whole story, however, yields different conclusions. Here are other data from the survey among retirees. It is not all about the money.

- Over 50% of retirees within the lowest net worth category (<$250,000) reported being completely or very satisfied with retirement. Even with lesser assets, satisfaction is more than possible.
- The level of retirement satisfaction was flat for those with any net worth greater than $1,000,000. More money made no difference.
- Stress levels and issues with relationships, health, loss of identity, and boredom impacted general satisfaction more than did net worth.

We are not asking you to ignore any anxiety you might have about finances, health, or any other concerns. We do ask, however, that for the sake of getting the most out of what follows in this chapter and the entire book, temporarily suspend your concerns and accept our contentions. With that acceptance, you can begin to discover the great possibilities of your retirement and how to reach that potential. Our objective is that when you have completed this book and revisit your concerns, you will find them significantly lessened.

Norwegian author and journalist, Arne Garborg (1851-1924), wrote, "For money you can have everything, it is said. No, that is not true. You can buy food, but not appetite; medicine, but not health; soft beds, but not sleep; knowledge, but not intelligence; glitter, but not comfort; fun, but not pleasure; acquaintances, but not friendship; servants, but not faithfulness; grey hair, but not honor; quiet days, but not peace. The shell of all things you can get for money. But not the kernel. That cannot be had for money."

Garborg's profound statement focused his insight on life in general, and that is surely appropriate. His words, however, may be even more applicable to retirement. If you embrace the notion that happiness in retirement is derived from the non-financial aspects, your level of anxiety will decrease.

There are two categories of retirees that can benefit from recognizing that retirement is not all about the money—those without substantial funds and those with substantial funds. If you have inferred from this statement that everyone can benefit, you are correct.

We are not so naïve as to believe money is not important. It is. There is no doubt that individuals and couples with different nest egg sizes may be doing different things in retirement. However, once you reach the threshold of financial security that matches your lifestyle or, perhaps, more importantly, you match your lifestyle to your financial means, the opportunities to live a fulfilling retirement are endless.

Later in this chapter, you will read Helen and Walt Devaney's story. They lived a fulfilling retirement life on social security and nominal wages from part time jobs. Their lives were meaningful, because most important to them were family, friends, and travel for which they found ways to do at minimal expense.

Keith Lawrence's parents, Howard and Patricia, are another example of a couple who lived a satisfying retirement with a modest income. They lived in rural New York, enjoyed family and friends, and traveled—paid for primarily by social security and selling Christmas trees.

You will also read about Joanne and Sam Sudman, a retired Florida couple who have above-average net worth, yet are living a fulfilling retirement primarily because they make decisions about how to best spend their time based on non-financial considerations; giving back to their community, connecting frequently with family and friends, trying new things to establish variety in their lives, and just having fun.

There are over 100,000 men across the country who continue to play what is referred to as "senior baseball." Many of these players are in their 50s, 60s, and beyond. They continue to play despite the inevitable aches and pains, because they are passionate about the game that they learned to love in their youth.

Some of the older players play as many as 100 games per year in local leagues and in tournaments around the country and the world.

They love the game and can afford the costs of travel and tournament fees. Most senior players, however, cannot afford to travel extensively to play. They play predominately in local leagues for fees that are typically less than $300 for the summer. The fees pay for two games per week all summer long, with perhaps a tournament or two thrown in. Therefore, for nominal league fees, gas money, and the cost of an occasional adult beverage after games, these players with less disposable income can and do also pursue their baseball passion as an integral component of their life plan.

Even with a smaller nest egg, you can pursue passions, connect with family and friends, give back to your community, continue to grow as an individual, and have fun. You can have a positive attitude about life, maintain your well-being, pursue your life purpose, live consistently with your core values, and have a plan that ensures all of these things come together in a meaningful way without great expenditure. Retirement life is far from being all about the money.

Secret 2: More Than Money
- Retirement is about much more than the money.
- The best things in life are not the things; plan your financial security, then focus on what really counts to you.

No Problem

Helen Young worked as a librarian and reared five children on her own after her first husband passed away at a very young age. After the children were all out of high school, Helen married her second husband, Walt Devaney, a truck driver. Between them, their retirement savings were meager. They owned their home in Toledo, Ohio, and were able to afford a very modest unit in a Florida trailer community, where they spent their retirement winters, until Helen passed away a few years ago.

Helen and Walt were passionate about three things; their family, their friends, and traveling, especially on cruises. If they could nurture these three passions, they would consider themselves to be living fully and having a fulfilling retirement. Their close and extended family visited often—so, no problem. They were at the social center of a wide circle of friends at their trailer community—so, no problem. They did not initially, however, seem to have the funds to travel as much as they would like.

Helen and Walt Devaney—ready for a cruise

But, again—no problem. Helen and Walt did two things—they chose to work part-time to supplement their social security income. Helen worked in the front office of their trailer community and Walt was the recreation director. In the summers, Walt umpired softball games around Toledo, staying close to the game he loved, sometimes up to five per day. They also began organizing cruises for their retirement community friends and others, making sure the groups were large enough for the cruise lines to give Helen and Walt their voyages for free.

Were they wealthy? By no means. Were they financially secure? Pretty much. But those are not the right questions to ask. The right question is, "Did they live fully and live a fulfilling retirement?"

The answer to that question, despite their modest net worth and their social security income, was "Yes." They found meaning in the things that cost them nothing, or, at least, very little. For Helen and Walt, the best things in retirement were free—family, relationships, and, through ingenuity and a little work (which they loved to do), their cruises.

Sam 24 by 7

Joanne and Sam Sudman live a full and fulfilling life in Sun City Center, Florida, having moved there from the Midwest as part of their retirement plan. They are fortunate to be financially secure and can be considered to have greater than average retirement funds. That being said, Joanne and Sam are a great example of how the meaning in their life is derived from decisions based on things other than finances. For the Sudmans, it is not about the money.

Sam had a diverse education and work career before retiring for the last of several times in 2005. He has a Bachelor's degree, four post-graduate degrees, including a Doctorate, and a certification in Nursing Home Administration. His early work life focused on using his education and passion for microbiology. He worked in and managed state public health laboratories in Ohio, Michigan, Tennessee, and Illinois.

Since 1978, Sam took a "quasi-sabbatical;" helped with the family business; bought a car leasing business, which he sold after seven years; retired; dove into a fulltime life as a community volunteer; went back to work with the Internal Revenue Service for eight years; and retired. Through much of this time, Sam was also spending one weekend each month in Chicago and two weeks each summer at camp to fulfill his obligation to the United States Army Reserves as a microbiologist. He retired from the Reserves in 1996, after 34 years.

Sam and Joanne Sudman

Joanne's career has been more consistent and it continues. She earned her Bachelor's and Master's in Speech Pathology, and with the exception of the times she had her children and during the Sudman's relocation to Florida, has worked in her field. She has been a speech and language pathologist in many venues, including Easter Seals, public and private schools, and in private practice. Since moving to Florida, Joanne has continued to work, albeit for three days a week.

Why does Joanne continue to work? It is not about the money. She loves the children with whom she works and knows that she is making a difference in their lives. The administration respects her for her experience and allows her the flexibility of working part time—she views it as a win-win situation.

She has begun to consider 2012 as her future retirement year. When asked what her biggest concern is as she looks forward to full retirement, she responds, "Being with Sam 24 by 7." Sam chimes in, "I have the same problem—being with Sam 24 by 7."

When she is not working, Joanne has discovered or rediscovered a number of interests, some which she does on her own and some with Sam. In many ways, she is practicing retirement. Joanne is getting to the gym more frequently; is Treasurer of the Ohio Club, a group of more than 500 former Ohio residents now living in Sun City Center; and is on the Board of Directors of her Congregation. She has also become passionate about crafting pottery.

With Sam, Joanne delivers Meals on Wheels; donates an evening each month to drive the community security patrol; and volunteers four times each month at the Tampa Performing Arts Center, which enables them to enjoy all of the entertainment that comes to the Center for free. As well as doing things together in the community, Joanne and Sam also visit their children and grandchildren in Philadelphia and Orlando as often as possible.

Sam is also active in the community. He is President of their homeowner's association; a member and former Treasurer of the Ohio Club; a dispatcher for the community emergency response squad; and a member of the local men's club, which is both a social and philanthropic organization. Sam is part of the men's club "Lifeline" program that installs emergency signal systems in the homes of residents who request them. Sam also continues to follow his microbiology passion, keeping his license current and taking continuing education courses.

There are three life plans at the Sudman's home, one for each of them as individuals and a shared plan. Perhaps the best example of their joint planning was their decision to move to Sun City Center. For ten years, they had been using their vacations to research places around the country they might choose to retire. They settled on

Florida and Sun City Center because their children and grandchildren are on the East Coast; they wanted a warm climate, but not a hot one; they wanted to be near water; and they wanted a community that was active, centrally located near academic, arts, culture, military, and religious opportunities, and one that had the facilities that would support them as they aged.

Joanne and Sam Sudman's lives are filled with their passions, friends and family, activities by which they give back to the community, personal growth, fun, and each other. While they have taken the steps to build financial security, how they choose to spend their time with meaning is not based on their finances.

For Helen, Walt, Joanne, Sam, and you, retirement is not all about the money.

Key Learning about "It's Not All about the Money"

1. Money is important to sustaining your lifestyle, but, regardless of your level of funds, it is not the primary source of happiness in retirement.
2. There are many ways to enjoy retirement life that cost little to nothing. A great retirement does not need to be expensive.

Getting Started

1. Think about and write down those things in your life that are currently a great source of happiness and satisfaction. Review them and notice how many are not reliant on significant funds. You can use the worksheet on the next page.
2. Think about the times in your life (e.g., your childhood, when you were in school, early in your career) when you were the most personally fulfilled. How much money did you have available to you at those times?
3. Take time to "stop and smell the roses," to recognize and appreciate the wonderful things you have in your life today. Create some new ways to enjoy them, to make them feel fresh and novel.

"It's Not All about the Money" Planning Worksheet

Personal Assessment: Rate the following statement from 1 to 5:

1 = This statement is far from describing the activities in my retirement life.

5 = This statement fully describes the activities in my retirement life.

"I can envision many meaningful activities in retirement life that will not be reliant on money."

Rating: 1   2   3   4   5

Personal thoughts about retirement not being all about the money:

_____

_____

_____

_____

_____

_____

_____

_____

_____

_____

The one person in my life who can best help me plan the non-financial aspects of my life is _____

Chapter 5

Stages of Retirement

"Retired is being twice tired, I've thought
First tired of working, Then tired of not.
Richard Armour

"The trouble with retirement is
that you never get a day off."
Abe Lemons

Do You Know?

The two most dangerous years in your life are the year you are born and the year you retire.

Retiring is as stressful as getting married, losing your job, or having a close family member become ill.

The number-one cause of disability in the world is depression. By 2020, depression is predicted to be the second leading cause of death. One-third of retirees suffer from depression at some point.

The highest suicide rate in the United States for any segment of the population is among men over 70; 50% higher than the suicide rate for teenagers. The speculation is that these men have lost their life purpose and their zest for living.

What are the "Stages of Retirement?"

These facts are alarming. Certainly, depression and suicide are among the more extreme reactions to an unfulfilling retirement, but the mere fact that some people get to that point highlights the need to be able to intervene before the risk gets too great. Understanding the five stages of retirement, how to recognize them, and how to respond to them will help you both continually move toward a fulfilling retirement and, importantly, minimize your risks.

The five stages of retirement are represented by the steps of the LifeScape Solutions™ model and the peak of the pyramid. The length of time people live in these stages and how deeply they feel them differs with the individual and how he or she has prepared and planned for retirement. Most people experience each of the five stages to some degree.

These are the five stages of retirement:

1. Anticipation—This is the stage that can start up to five years before retirement. Your opportunity is to use this stage to begin creating your plan as early as possible to minimize the amount of time and energy wasted and to maximize your productivity at work and the quality of your life. This plan will also make the transition into retirement as seamless as possible and your journey to a fulfilling retirement as quick as possible. You likely feel a lot of excitement and hopefulness through this stage, as well as some level of anxiety and discomfort. The end of the anticipation stage is the retirement event itself—some have called it the "big day." The next day, you will not go to work, at least not the work that has likely been your primary career for some time.

2. Honeymoon—You are now retired and it is great. You have the freedom to do what you want to do; to just be you. No alarm clock, no business attire, no rush-hour drive—you are elated and enthusiastic and feel a sense of relief, independence, and discovery. Many retirees are in the honeymoon stage up to two

years. For some, however, the honeymoon is short.

3. Disenchantment—The honeymoon is over. You may still be doing the things that you were doing during the honeymoon stage, but you are now asking yourself, "Is this all there is?" A typical example we often hear goes something like this. "When I retired, I envisioned playing golf every day, and that is exactly what I did. It was great, but after about six months, I realized that I was no longer energized to get going in the morning and get out to the course. It was then I realized that golf was really all I was doing. There has to be more than that."

You will know you are in Disenchantment when you feel letdown, loneliness, boredom, or disappointment; you may even be depressed. Some estimates are that 30% of retirees experience some level of depression over the years. The Disenchantment stage lasts varying lengths of time, and individuals can move in and out of it as life circumstances change. Sadly, some people get into Disenchantment and never get out. We want to help this never happen to you.

4. Rejuvenation—This is the stage in which you take stock of your situation and climb out of disenchantment. You are adapting to the reality of retirement and how it is affecting you. You are discovering what makes you happy and satisfied; what brings meaning to your life. You feel reenergized and engaged. If you develop and implement your plan before you retire (during the Anticipation stage), you can minimize or, perhaps, even avoid the Disenchantment stage, feeling continually revitalized.

5. Fulfillment—This is your ultimate retirement goal—a life filled with connectedness, giving back, pursuing your passions, personal growth, and fun. Your attitude about life is positive; you have taken the steps to keep your energy high; you have matched your lifestyle to your available resources; and you are in touch with your life purpose and core values. Importantly, you have a plan that is the first step toward keeping you fulfilled.

Our objective is to help you develop a retirement plan, know how to implement it, and know how to keep it fresh throughout your retirement years to minimize the time you spend in the Disenchantment stage and maximize the time you spend in the Fulfillment stage.

Secret 3: Quest
- Retirement is a journey with five distinct stages; and some people get stuck.
- Understand them, know which stage you are in, and know how to move forward.

The Lives of Others

Throughout Ross Love's life, despite career changes and experiencing the stages of retirement, he has steadfastly maintained a constancy of purpose. Over his 28-year corporate career, Ross rose through the brand management organization and was appointed Vice President-Advertising, Procter & Gamble Worldwide, where for ten years, he led the marketing organization of the world's leading advertiser. In 1995, he began a transition from a corporate to an entrepreneurial career when he purchased his first radio station and a year later left P&G to start a broadcasting company. He built Blue Chip Broadcasting into a 20-station group across six cities, the second largest African-American owned radio broadcasting company in the country.

Ross Love

During and after his corporate and entrepreneurial careers, Ross has understood and followed his life purpose, which he states as, "doing things that make a positive difference in the lives of others." While at P&G, Ross started and led The Partnership for a Drug-Free America's initiative that developed virtually all of the anti-drug messages targeted to the African-American community. As Chairman of the Association of National Advertisers, he worked with the media industry and the Clinton Administration to adopt the first program content ratings for television, and he began the dialogue within the advertising industry regarding the need for and business value of more diversity.

As majority owner and CEO of the broadcasting company, he infused his core value of civic responsibility into the values of the company and its employees. Under Ross's guidance, the radio stations focused on making a difference in their communities as much as focusing on the bottom line. The stations recognized "the Whiz Kid of the Week" to promote the importance of young black students engaging in their own education, honored the "African-American Business of the Month" and encouraged listeners to patronize these businesses, contracted to run Cincinnati's Black Family Reunion to promote family values in the community, and ran advertising campaigns to help address gang violence. His company also purchased Cincinnati's Jazz Festival, an annual community institution that was in danger of being shut down, and filled the need for a new major sponsor to help sustain the Kentucky Derby Festival's "Thunder over Louisville," the nation's largest fireworks display.

When the company was sold, Ross took the highly unusual step of granting bonuses typically equivalent to a year's pay or more as a "thank you" to every employee who had put several years into making the venture a success. Again, he was making a difference in the lives of others.

The sale of the company could be viewed as Ross's retirement, and immediately thereafter, his life went in two different directions. One journey kept him on focus to his life purpose. The other led to a period of unhappiness from which Ross needed to extract himself.

In April 2001, a 19-year old black male was shot and killed by a Cincinnati police officer during a foot pursuit. A week after the shooting, a group of 200 citizens, including the victim's mother, interrupted a city council meeting demanding accountability for the death. A series of events led to a full-blown riot breaking out that evening and continuing for several nights. Ross Love was at home listening to news of the rioting. He immediately knew the possible implications to the city. Instead of bemoaning the situation, he took action that would consume much of the next three years of his life.

Within 24 hours, Ross convened a group of African-American civic leaders and professionals and guided their development of a proposal on what to do to respond to the unrest, focusing on meaningful action that would address the root causes. Before taking the proposal to the city, they convened the CEO's of the top companies in the city. The corporate leaders supported this initiative when Ross made the proposal to the mayor.

The actions that were implemented—from major early childhood initiatives to real changes in policing practices to programs addressing gang violence reduction and the chronically unemployed. The programs have proven to be substantial and sustainable—creating systematic changes that reduced racial disparities and making a real difference in the lives of literally thousands of people in need.

As the community effort was taking hold, Ross returned to the business world by investing in several companies over several years, but soon found himself burdened with an unhappiness he could not put his finger on. Over the course of months, he had what he calls a "spiritual dialogue," eventually discovering the source of the unhappiness. Ross realized that while his community efforts were very satisfying, his business ventures were not. He found himself involved in business simply because "that's what he does," and that was not satisfying. It was not consistent with his life purpose and core values. Ross refocused his business involvement, deciding that he should only bring his business skills to bear to make a difference in the lives of others.

Ross is now active with two companies. One has developed a device that has the potential to save literally hundreds of thousands of lives. The device helps personnel in hospital emergency departments and EMS vehicles place EKG probes on the patient with greater accuracy, insuring better diagnosis and proper, faster treatment; improving survival rates for heart attack patients. The other is a cosmetics company that focuses on empowering women of color to see their outer beauty and their inner strength, helping them define their own lives with greater confidence and self-esteem. Ross's business ventures are aligned with his life purpose.

He has also continued to find ways to give back to his community. He chaired the group that developed a new strategy for the local United Way, focusing the allocation of funds on the most important community needs, children and employment. He also chaired the United Way Board of Directors. Ross was one of the prime movers of the Cincinnati Initiative to Reduce Violence, a program that yielded a meaningful reduction in homicides among chronically violent street groups in a way that enabled the former gang members to build new futures.

Ross would tell you that his life has created a stream of both personal joy and fulfillment, and that deep spiritual reflection has helped enable course corrections at critical junctures to keep him working on the things that that are consistent with what he cares most about. He would also tell you that he learned about halfway through his life that the true measure of a person is not related to the blessings, small or large, with which they have been endowed, but rather how they are used in the betterment of those they can touch.

Multi-National

Peter Schmid was the kind of leader that everyone admired and felt fortunate to be able to work with—full of zest, quick to laugh, dedicated to helping others, and constructively inquisitive. After nine years of retirement, a few bumps in the road, and a few gray hairs later, he retains these characteristics. He and his wife, Marina, originally of Rome, Italy, have been living a multi-national retirement that is centered on what is truly important to them.

Peter Schmid

Peter began to anticipate and plan for retirement three years before the big event. He had a successful career full of challenge, personal growth, fun, and excitement. However, as the experience became less personally satisfying, he decided it was time to try something new. Being a true professional, he shared his retirement plans with his leadership well in advance to facilitate a smooth transition.

Prior to retiring, Peter engaged experts, including a financial advisor, to help him ensure a successful transition into his next chapter of life. In the process, he also assessed what additional skills might be required to enhance his future experience. As an example, he recognized that he had never acquired fundamental computer skills and reached out to his highly competent secretary to teach him the necessary basics.

Because of his planning and his willingness to recognize the value of experts, Peter encountered neither transition issues nor regrets. He closed the door on the career phase of his life and never looked back, sliding nicely into the honeymoon stage of retirement.

Peter and Marina immediately purchased an apartment in Spiez, Switzerland, Peter's home town. They envisioned it as a base for future vacations, travel, and visits to Marina's Rome-based family. Shortly thereafter, however, Peter's mother became seriously ill, and his first retirement year was dedicated to her care and comfort. He viewed it as a true blessing that retirement allowed him the extra time to spend with her before she passed away.

Following his mother's passing, Peter found himself, really for the first time, dealing with retirement. In the absence of a routine or rhythm, he found himself somewhat disoriented, and recognized the necessity for making firm plans for the new reality. Peter's and Marina's important first decision was to split their time between the United States, where they had family and friends, and Switzerland, with its beloved mountains and lakes and its proximity of Marina's family. The "part-time vacation home" turned into a "permanent second home."

Peter's new plan also included "giving something back." He felt the need and obligation to return to others the many blessings he had. An opportunity presented itself when volunteers from a local charity, Valley Interfaith Food & Clothing Center, requested his assistance in formulating its first ever strategic plan. That exercise evolved into a serious long-term commitment, including serving a six-year term as the charity's President and doing a number of hands-on projects like rewriting the "Volunteer Handbook."

The personal satisfaction Peter gains from giving back and the decision to live a multi-national lifestyle rejuvenated his retirement. Peter and Marina find themselves having to be "true Europeans" for the first time in their adult life. While both are of European origin, they have found the experience of being "residents" rather than "visitors" intellectually challenging. It has provided them the opportunity to gain a real-life appreciation of their cultural heritage by simply living their daily lives in a completely different environment. In addition to meeting new friends and neighbors, rediscovering old friendships, enjoying the incredible beauty of their surroundings, and being closer to Marina's family, they are also enjoying the simple discoveries of life. For instance, on one of their hikes through the Alps, they came across a herd of cows. Peter wondered why some cows have larger bells than others. When they came upon the farmer, Peter asked how the decision was made to award a given cow the larger bell. The farmer replied, "The cows make the decision. They choose the lead cow, and we give her the larger bell."

This seemingly small incident is but one example of Peter's spontaneity and curiosity and of his personal philosophy to keep learning and remain intellectually challenged. He closely adheres to his mother's admonishment, "Use it or lose it." While his current life-style, his interaction with his daughters and their families, including six grandsons, and his continuing charitable activity provide a great deal of stimulation, Peter feels a need to continue to expand his horizons. He has taken up being a "sous chef" to his very talented spouse-chef, and enjoys shopping for the ingredients for his creations. He is also immersed in a Georgetown University (his alma mater) DVD course on Philosophy, Religion and the Meaning of Life. As Peter says, "I'm keeping my little grey cells as active as I can."

Peter has travelled across the ocean and through the stages of retirement. He anticipated the transition, had an all-too-brief honeymoon stage, experienced a degree of disorientation, took steps to rejuvenate his plans, and is living a fulfilling retirement. When asked what his retirement journey of nearly a decade has taught him, and what he would pass on to others, Peter responded with a simple, yet profound list:

1. Carpe Diem; embrace every opportunity
2. Use it or lose it; stay intellectually active
3. Give of yourself; share your God-given gifts freely
4. Shake it up; get out of the rut; variety in life is essential
5. Don't wait to live your dreams; make them a current reality
6. Lean into opportunities; even misfortune generates new possibilities
7. Don't wait for the call; reach out and contact a friend

Key Learning about "Stages of Retirement"

1. Retirement is a major life transition and its stages are predictable. Most prospective retirees anticipate the "big day," but rarely beyond to what is next.
2. Everyone proceeds through the five stages of retirement, but each at his or her own pace. Some get bogged down in Disenchantment and, as a result, never get the opportunity to completely experience a fulfilling retirement.
3. There are actions you can take at each stage to maximize your enjoyment of the journey and move you toward fulfillment.

Getting Started

1. Establish which stage you are in now and, therefore, what the next stage will be. Discuss your assessment with a good friend or family member. Consider whether you have the right plans in place with regards to your stage.
2. Think about other changes that have occurred in your life. What has it taught you about how you manage transition? What works best for you? What did not work? You can capture your thoughts on the worksheet on the next page.

"Stages of Retirement" Planning Worksheet

The stage of retirement I am currently in is (circle one):

Anticipation   Honeymoon   Disenchantment

Rejuvenation   Fulfillment

Personal thoughts about the stages of retirement, where I am currently, and what I have learned from other life transitions:

_____

_____

_____

_____

_____

_____

_____

_____

_____

_____

_____

_____

The one person in my life who can best help me assess the stage of retirement I am in is _____

Chapter 6

Planning
Retirement

*"Planning is bringing the future into the present
so you can do something about it now."*
Alan Lakein

*"Life is what happens to you while you're
busy making other plans."*
John Lennon

Do You Know?

It has been consistently demonstrated that having a plan is among the most important habits of the most successful retirees.

Those who have a game plan, both for fiscal and non-fiscal aspects, and who frequently revisit and update that plan are most satisfied with their retirement lives.

Many people spend more time planning a two-week vacation than they do planning their retirement.

"He who fails to plan, plans to fail." (proverb)

What is "Planning Retirement?"

The word "plan" may conjure up overwhelming images of disciplined military campaigns, rigorous corporate projects, or massive real estate developments. If so, the concept of planning for retirement could be daunting. You might ask, "Do I really want to spend my whole retirement planning my retirement?" Of course, that is not what we have in mind. We do have in mind, however, that planning is critical to how fulfilling your retirement will be.

Think differently about the word "plan." Conjure images of planning for your wedding, for your last vacation, or for the project to modernize your kitchen. You knew instinctively that for each of those and many other large and small projects and events in your life, planning would be the key to success.

This chapter begins the planning approach that will be a key to success for your retirement. It is important to recognize early in the process that just as each person's fingerprints are unique, so is his or her retirement. For that reason, you will not find a prescription for your personal plan. Rather, you will find a framework for considering the key elements that comprise a fulfilling retirement. Your plan, therefore, will best fit your interests, be aligned with who you are, and be consistent with your particular life circumstances.

In his poem, *Desiderata*, Max Ehrmann asserted:

> *If you compare yourself with others, you may become vain and bitter; for always there will be greater and lesser persons than yourself.*

> *Enjoy your achievements as well as your plans. Keep interested in your own career, however humble; it is a real possession in the changing fortunes of time.*

Replace the word "career" with "retirement," and thank you, Mr. Ehrmann. Each of us has the opportunity to create our best plan. In this chapter, you will see an example of how one retirement plan came to be. The intent for sharing the plan is not to say that it should be yours, but rather to give you a feeling for an approach you can use and to help you envision both your planning and your retirement future.

Secret 4: Planning
- Retirement is exciting, but also unnerving, causing some to hesitate to think about and plan for their future.
- Create a holistic plan before you retire to reduce the anxiety and increase the odds of a fulfilling retirement.

Alan's Story

(Keith Lawrence) By the time my friend and co-author, Alan Spector, retired in 2002, he had put together a personal plan that positioned him to have a robust life-after-career. Over the years, I have watched him live out his plan as well as modify it as his life circumstances have changed.

During that time, I have been in a position to interact with hundreds of future and current retirees. My observation is that

Alan has it figured out better than anyone I have encountered. As I researched and planned for my own retirement, I built into my approach what I learned from Al and his experiences.

In this chapter, Alan will share his personal retirement planning story with you. Based on his story and our extensive research, we have established a practical, yet thorough approach for you to consider using as you proceed with your own planning. Later in the chapter, we will share that approach with you, and it will become the basis upon which you can best use the remainder of the book. At the end, you will have completed your initial retirement plan and learned how to keep it fresh as your life circumstances change.

Baseball and Books

(Alan Spector) I was furiously riding my bike on a typically hot, humid summer St. Louis morning in 1956, heading toward Fogarty Park, which shared land with our Daniel Boone Elementary School, about ten minutes from my house. My baseball glove was slung over a handle bar. My well-worn baseball was stuffed into the pocket of my baggy "wear-your-old-jeans-to-play-ball" pants.

The sound of a baseball card slapping against the spokes of my coaster added to the familiarity of the ride—a ride I had made hundreds of times—a ride that would again connect me with fellow baseball fanatics and friends, Marc Golubock, Steve Novack, Jackie Mercurio, and others.

Mom had kissed and hugged me and sent me off into my day with her usual admonition, "Have a good time and don't do anything to hurt anyone."

That was the extent to which Mom managed my ten-year-old day. The rest was up to my friends and me. We chose the bat-and-ball game we would play that day based on the number of guys who showed up. Would it be a full game of baseball or rounds or Indian ball or cork ball or hit-the-bat? We picked sides, resolved disputes, cared for injuries, changed games as players came and went throughout the day, and got home for lunch or dinner or whenever we were required, mostly on time. There were no adults around, just us. We learned initiative, compromise, self-sufficiency, and planning.

I was passionate about baseball. If the game had a bat and a ball, I would play it, all day.

I had supper that evening with my family in our small kitchen, in which Mom, Dad, my two sisters, Carol and Marti, and I barely fit around the table. After dinner, it was back outside to play a neighborhood-wide game of hide-and-go-seek.

When it grew too dark to play, I was back inside and ready to settle in with a book, perhaps *Ojibway Drums* or *Gene Rhodes, Cowboy* or *Miss Pickerall Goes to Mars*, each a favorite selection from the "Weekly Reader Book Club." I was passionate about books. If it had words on a page, I would read it, all evening.

Why relate the story of my typical ten-year-old day? Fast forward—I am 64 years old and have been retired for eight years. I am still playing baseball; and you are reading the third book I have written since retiring. While I have many other activities which I enjoy and find meaningful, I am fortunate to also be pursuing the passions of my youth.

All this has not been accidental. Playing baseball, writing, and my other pursuits are part of an ever-evolving plan. As we enter the section of the book in which you will develop your plan, allow me to share my retirement planning journey with you. Many of the principles you will find employed throughout the book were derived from my approach and experiences, subsequently supported by research and the experiences of others.

The Journey Begins

By 1997, I was 28 years into my career with the Procter & Gamble Company. I was fortunate in that I was still energized to get up each morning and go to work, because I enjoyed what I was doing and who I was working with. International business and travel were integral to my responsibilities, ensuring that I continued to grow and develop as an employee and as a person. I was putting in 12 to 14 hour days and averaging a little more than a week every month outside the country on business.

Despite that workload, I had time to play some softball and get to the gym regularly, and, my wife, Ann, and I were able to travel reasonably often, something we loved to do. We were busy socially in Cincinnati and had a chance to see relatives and friends throughout the year in St. Louis, in the Northeast, and elsewhere.

Ann managed the Mathematics Tutoring Lab at a branch of the

University of Cincinnati and was doing some private math tutoring in our home. Our children had graduated from college, were out on their own, and had begun to build the solid foundations of their independent lives.

We were fortunate to be living an enjoyable and reasonably balanced life. Also by 1997, I had my AARP card, and Ann was nearing 50. My work colleagues who were five to ten years older than I were making the decision to retire. It became clear that it was time for us to start considering retirement and begin our planning process. We had no specific timing in mind, but based on when others were retiring, we set our sights on 55, knowing we could always change our minds later.

The next five years would be a period of continuing to work, beginning to envision our future, establishing a plan, and, as it turns out, practicing retirement. To get started on the journey, I began to do some research by interviewing recent retirees. What had they learned? What were the key factors in their decision? What was working for them and what was not? Were there any surprises, positive or negative? What were the secrets?

The Three (Four) Questions

One afternoon, I was at the airport to begin a business trip and pleased to run into a former boss, Peter Graham, who had retired a few years earlier. I asked Peter how retirement was going and told him that I was trying to decide when to retire.

Peter smiled and said, "The decision of when to retire is an easy one. All you have to do is ask three questions, and when the answer to each one is 'yes,' it's time to retire."

"OK, Peter, what are the questions?"

"Simple. Do you have enough? Will you have enough to do? Have you had enough?"

I immediately knew that these simple yet profound questions would guide the remainder of my retirement decision making and planning.

"Do we have enough?"

Like many, our first consideration was the state of our finances. We had been proactive and engaged a financial advisor a decade earlier—long enough to know our first choice of advisors was the wrong one. By 1997, we had switched to the advisor we still have today.

Ann and I had already been tracking our spending; we knew where our money was going and why. We used that information to project what we believed our retirement spending would be in four categories: general living, home/auto, travel, and gifting. We then asked ourselves what we would spend if we really splurged and what we would spend if we needed to be more conservative.

We took each of these spending plans to our financial advisor, who worked out the details to help us answer the question, "Will we have enough?" His analysis said, "Yes."

Despite this rigorous data-based approach and the help of trusted experts, we found it an emotional decision as well. It is not easy to say that in some number of years, we will stop working, stop collecting a pay check, and begin living on our savings. We needed more than the data.

One summer evening, Ann and I packed a picnic, went to a local park, and found a secluded table under the protective arms of a cooling shade tree. We ate our picnic and talked through all of our potential financial scenarios. All of the data lined up, but it took two hours of discussion to get through the anxiety of the decision. We looked each other in the eyes, held hands, and answered, "Yes, we will have enough."

"Will I have enough to do?"

To answer this question, I broke it down into two parts—what activities/pursuits would I want to be doing, and would I be healthy and fit enough to do them for as long as I would be retired?

I gained an additional insight as I interviewed retirees and asked them what had surprised them. Many shared a common theme that warranted attention. Although they phrased their answers differently, what they consistently said was that they found it important and difficult to replace the intellectual stimulation they had taken for granted at work. Fitness, which I was initially thinking of just as physical fitness, now had a mental fitness component as well.

Following these interviews and a great deal of introspection, I used these planning categories: health, physical fitness, mental fitness, family, friends, travel, athletics, and volunteering. For some activities, I would merely need to continue to do what I had been doing all along, like having annual physicals and eye examinations and semi-annual dental exams. For some activities, I would need to start anew, like finding places to volunteer my time, skills, and resources to make a difference for others.

I also realized that many choices would fall into more than one category, perhaps being the activities about which I was or would be most passionate. For example, I have always enjoyed working out at the gym and had studied the best methods for doing so. I had also been observing the aging process of my loved ones and not liking what I saw as they became less active far too soon. Thus, one element of my initial plan was to become a certified Personal Trainer and volunteer my time with senior citizens to help them gain and maintain their physical fitness, thereby enhancing their quality of life.

I completed the activities lists for each of my categories—the result was a holistic and satisfying plan. I was confident that I would be living fully and living a fulfilling life when I retired. Each activity category had a list of pursuits that I was sure would make a difference to me and to others. I was still years away from retiring, but I had a plan and began working to implement it. Over those years, I learned a valuable lesson that I should have realized from the beginning—the plan would be ever-changing and that was fine. My activities plan on retirement day was different from the one I developed at age 50, and it has been constantly changing ever since.

As John Bolton, a former colleague, used to say, "A plan is only something from which to deviate." His message was, basically, have a plan, then modify it as circumstances change—and they will change.

I had a plan and answered, "Yes, I will have enough to do."

"Have I had enough?"

For me, this turned out to be the hardest "yes" to achieve. I was blessed to have enjoyed work. Even on my last day, I was still going strong at 6:00pm. For many, answering "yes" to this question comes first—not for me. Yet I knew, as the time approached, that 33 years was a long and sufficient career. However, it was really the attraction of my plan for the other side of retirement day that allowed me to answer, "Yes, I had enough."

I was ready to move on. The answer to all three questions was yes. When I shared the concept of the three questions with my friend, Keith Lawrence, however, he suggested a fourth. It may have been offered tongue-in-cheek, but it is not a trivial question. "Is your spouse (partner) excited about your new and different future together?"

Ann and I were looking forward to spending more time together, as my hours at work and extensive travel had often made that difficult. Yet, Ann had retired one year before I did and had developed a retirement life of her own.

My late Uncle Norman, who had been my mentor throughout my life, once talked to me about this subject when he was describing retirement to me. He began the discussion by saying, "I married your Aunt Leah for love and for life, but not for lunch."

What Uncle Norman meant was that while he wanted to spend a lot of time with her, Aunt Leah and he also needed to spend time apart, doing their own thing.

Ann and I had shared in the development of both our separate and mutual plans and were looking forward to a shared retirement. But we decided to run an experiment. We predicted its success; nevertheless, experiment we did.

We planned a winter car trip to San Antonio, Texas; three days driving down, three days in San Antonio, and three days back. Part of our retirement plan was to travel extensively, and we knew a lot of the travel would be by car. How would it go? Would we enjoy extensive travel time together, a large part of which would be cooped up in a car? Would we be as excited about that prospect after the trip as before it?

The trip was an unqualified success. We had met question four head on and answered, "Yes, my spouse was excited about our new and different future together."

I retired in early May 2002.

"...From Which To Deviate"

The attraction of traveling more in retirement caused Ann and me to think differently about our preretirement years. We developed what we called "practicing retirement." Why wait until retirement day to focus on things we loved to do? You never know what tomorrow may bring.

We started what we called the "vacation-of-the-month club" and began planning a trip each month. To be clear, this did not mean we were about to begin taking lavish and long vacations each month. Neither our finances nor work schedules would allow that. We did plan one or two nice vacations each year, but we also took day trips within driving distance of our home in Cincinnati. We created some long weekends to drive to St. Louis, where many of our relatives and high school friends lived. We extended holiday weekends and drove to visit relatives in the Northeast. Occasionally, Ann would join me on a business trip.

We maximized our vacation time and managed expenses by driving versus flying and by staying with relatives. But, we were practicing retirement by planning for and enjoying our travel.

The idea of practicing retirement led in other directions as well. When I first built my plan, I had included continuing to play softball in local leagues. I enjoyed the camaraderie and competition, but deep down, something was missing. For me, softball is not baseball, a true passion of my youth and, as it turns out, one that remains today.

In February 2000, I had the opportunity to attend a Cincinnati Reds baseball fantasy camp. During the camp, another player from Cincinnati invited me to play on his senior baseball team back home. I jumped at the chance.

This was another opportunity to practice retirement. Shortly thereafter, I was playing about 75 games each year in local leagues and in tournaments around the country, many in Florida and annually in Cooperstown. Baseball was also another reason to travel. In fact, at the end of the month I retired, Ann and I traveled with a group from all across the United States to Beijing, China to play baseball against locals and to sightsee.

We had launched our travel and baseball passions before we retired and have continued them ever since.

Just as my reintroduction to baseball changed my plan, so have ever-changing life circumstances caused us to reassess and renew. Since developing our first plan, we have had four grandchildren; Jordan and Aaron live in St. Louis, and Jake and Zoe live in Boston. Elder relatives have gone through illnesses, needing significant support, and some have passed away. Meaningful volunteer opportunities have come our way. The stock market experienced its steepest loss since the Great Depression. I hurt my back and spent months in rehab. Playing senior baseball prompted me to write and publish my first book about the experience, taking my passion for books in a new and different direction. Keith Lawrence convened the foursome that would become LifeScape Solutions™ and prompt the writing of this book. And, last but not least, we have moved "home" to St. Louis after being away for 40+ years.

These changes in life circumstances and others, some planned, others not, have each caused me to reassess my plan and to modify it accordingly. I found it much easier to deal with life changes knowing that I had a base plan on which to build. When I hurt my back and my baseball future was in doubt, it was clearly disappointing. But I knew there were many other things that I was doing and could do to continue to have a fulfilling life. When I recovered and was able to return to baseball, it felt like a bonus.

I expect life circumstances to continue to change, and I expect these changes to prompt renewal of my plan. I also expect that periodically, I will reassess and renew my plan, even if I am not confronted by significant life changes. "A plan is only something from which to deviate."

The New Question Two

Before we move on to discuss our planning model with you, let us revisit the three basic questions you can use to decide when to retire. 1) Do you have enough? 2) Will you have enough to do? 3) Have you had enough?

Our interviews, research, and personal experiences have caused us to restate question two, "Do you have a holistic plan, and do you know how to implement it and keep it fresh over time?"

Helping you answer the restated question is, in essence, an objective of this book and the basis for the planning approach we will explain and guide you through.

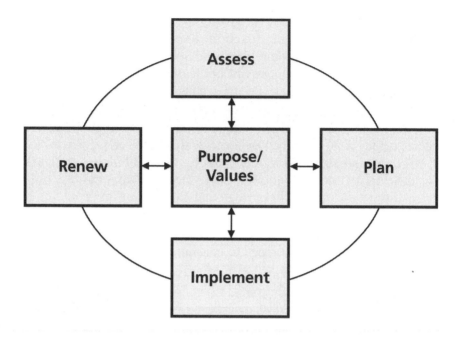

The overall model and the activities within the model are based on proven techniques, which we will share with you in more detail in their respective chapters. These are the key components of the planning model:

- **Assess:** The best way to start on your plan is to determine where you are in your life today versus where you would like to be. This is why we have included assessment statements on the worksheets at the end of the chapters. When you candidly rate yourself, you will, in essence, be developing your first assessment.

- **Plan:** Based on your personal assessment, there are things in your life that you will want to start doing, stop doing, and continue doing. You will be introduced to our Start-Stop-Continue approach before the next chapter, then use it in Chapters 7 through 17 as you begin to make the individual choices that will establish your retirement plan.

- **Implement:** Having a plan, but doing nothing with it, is the same as not having a plan. Chapter 18, "Doing What You Planned," will address what it takes to implement your personal life plan and best manage the changes you will be making in your life.

- **Renew:** Life circumstances inevitably change. A good plan is one that is modified to take these life changes, whether positive or negative, into account. Chapter 19, "Renewing Your Plan," will share an approach to help you keep your plan fresh over time.
- **Purpose/Values:** The most fulfilling retirement will occur when your plans are consistent with your life purpose and your core values. Purpose and values, in themselves a key element of a fulfilling retirement, will guide every choice you make as you plan your retirement and implement and renew your plan. Chapter 7 will help you begin to reflect on and articulate your personal purpose and values.

Using the planning model is not a one-time thing. Rather it is an iterative process to keep the plan up to date as you move clockwise around the model represented in the diagram. When you have completed the first round through the model, you will have the confidence and experience to be able to answer "Yes" to the new question two, "Do you have a holistic plan, and do you know how to implement it and keep it fresh over time?"

Key Learning about "Planning Retirement"

1. To be most successful, retirement, just as all significant changes (e.g., getting married, moving to a new home, losing weight) requires a plan.
2. Your plan is not cast in stone. However, it is your foundation when life circumstances change; the plan is only something from which to deviate.
3. Begin to live your plan today to realize your dreams sooner and to learn a lot about how to improve your plan over time.

Getting Started

1. Think about yourself and your feelings about planning. Have you made and used plans in your life (e.g., finding a new job,

preparing for a vacation, helping your child determine which college to attend)? Do you like to plan? If not, what steps could you take to be more likely to develop a retirement plan (e.g., identify a friend or family member who is a good planner to get you started)?

2. If you are not yet retired, candidly answer the four questions to help you decide when you should retire. If you are already retired, also candidly answer the questions. Doing so will help guide the remainder of your planning.

   a. Do I have enough?

   b. Do I have a holistic retirement plan?

   c. Have I had enough?

   d. Is my partner excited about our new and different future together?

"Planning Retirement" Worksheet

Personal Assessment: Rate the following statement from 1 to 5:
1 = This statement in no way describes my view about planning.
5 = This statement fully describes my view about planning.

"I understand the value of planning and am committed to developing my retirement plan."

Rating: 1 2 3 4 5

Personal thoughts about planning for retirement:

_____

_____

_____

_____

_____

_____

_____

_____

Do I have enough?   Yes   No
Do I have a holistic retirement plan? Yes   No
Have I had enough? Yes   No
Is my partner excited about our new and different
future together? Yes No

The one person in my life who can best help me implement the immediate next step of planning for retirement is

_____

Embrace The Journey

The first section of the book helped you envision *Your Retirement Quest.* This section will help you embrace the journey by understanding the key elements of a fulfilling retirement and beginning to make the informed choices that are right for you to build your personal plan.

In Chapters 7 through 15, we will detail each of the key elements. Importantly, each of the chapters will have worksheets, although these will be somewhat different than those you have already used. Instructions on how to best use the key element worksheets are on pages 94 to 96.

Before proceeding, it will be helpful to review the LifeScape Solutions™ model and its key elements.

Secret 5: Holistic

- There are 10 critical areas that make up a fulfilling retirement; many of them are overlooked.
- You will live fully when you embrace each of the key elements in your life.

These are the foundation building blocks and other key elements of the model:

LifeScape Plan: a practical and holistic approach to achieving your dreams in retirement

Well-Being: the energy to live fully today and throughout your retirement

Financial Security: matching your lifestyle to your financial resources

Purpose/Values: your reason for being and what is truly important to you in life

Attitude: the mindset with which you approach life and meet the challenges and opportunities of retirement

Connectedness: initiating and nurturing the many relationships that are important in life

Giving Back: making a valuable contribution to others (friends, family, community, world); being part of something greater than yourself

Passions: activities that give you a sense of energy, provide you with a sense of achievement, and play to your strengths

Growth: being mentally stimulated with new activities, learning, and challenges to keep your life fresh and exciting

Fun: drawing excitement, pleasure, recreation, and satisfaction from life

After sharing these key elements in more detail, we will address how to consider the effect your retirement will have on those around you. Then we will help you bring it all together—you will leave this section of the book with your initial personal retirement plan.

Chapter 7

Purpose
and Values

*"It is not hard to make decisions when
you know what your values are."*
Roy Disney

*"Good luck is another name
for tenacity of purpose."*
Ralph Waldo Emerson

Do You Know?

Only 20% of people in a worldwide survey of all age groups answered that they "certainly knew the purpose of life." In the same survey, only 5% said they thought "everyone" or "most people" know the purpose of life.

Those who are driven by inner purpose, versus those driven by external demands and rewards, are more creative, have higher levels of confidence, and experience more excitement in life.

Per bestselling author, Jim Collins, "Very few companies succeed over time. Those that enjoy enduring success have a core purpose and values that remain fixed-while their strategies and practices endlessly adapt to a changing world."

What are "Purpose and Values?"

Life purpose and personal values are vital building blocks for a fulfilling retirement and a central component of our planning model. They help guide you as you seek to determine how you want to best spend your time, energy, and resources. They also serve to help you know whether you are living the fulfilling life you desire. Living to your life purpose and according to your values should bring you happiness, satisfaction, and fulfillment. The 16th century French Renaissance writer Michel de Montaigne wrote, "The great and glorious masterpiece of man is to know how to live to purpose."

Futurist, author, architect, and inventor, Buckminster Fuller died in 1983, nearing his 88th birthday. When he was a young husband and father, his six-year old daughter died of complications from polio and spinal meningitis. Although medical practices at the time could do little to save her, Fuller blamed himself and entered a period of drinking, isolation, and thoughts of suicide. As he came out of his malaise, he began a philosophical search for his purpose in life. Fuller concluded that his purpose was to add value to and improve the quality of people's lives on earth. He made it his life's work to discover how much one person could contribute to changing the world and benefitting humanity.

As Fuller further refined his life philosophy, he developed his concept of "precession." Fuller described precession as when an action creates a meaningful side effect—his best analogy being that of a bee collecting nectar to take back to the hive for the production of honey. Nectar collection is the bee's goal, and through satisfaction of its instinctive programming, it gets positive feedback from the universe when that goal is accomplished.

Fuller observed, however, that the bee's life purpose is something different than collecting nectar and making honey. Rather, the bee's purpose is to cross-pollinate flowers to help sustain life on earth. Cross-pollination is a side effect of the bee's activity or goal. The bee is not thinking about its role of sustaining life on earth. It is thinking about nectar and honey.

Like the bee, you may have activities and goals that are more achievable, more near-term, more specific, and less grandiose than achieving your life's purpose. But, Fuller would argue, if your activities are well-chosen, the side effects will be to move you toward your life purpose. Then, like the bee, you will get positive feedback from the universe.

Regardless of your life purpose, if your activities have the effect of adding value as you perceive it, happiness, satisfaction, and fulfillment will follow. Said another way, activities chosen to be consistent with achieving your purpose will enable you to live a full and fulfilling life.

Personal values, like life purpose, play a role in how you feel about yourself and how you affect others. Your values most meaningfully reflect your core beliefs and philosophy, and, whether you have articulated them to yourself or not, they guide your behavior and affect your level of happiness. If, for example, integrity is one of your personal values, you will find it difficult to be dishonest, and, if you do something dishonestly, it will bother you, perhaps for a long time. Another example comes from the relationship of employees to their company. If an employee works for a company that shares his or her core values, he or she is more likely to be happier and more productive at work.

Similar to life purpose, if you choose your retirement activities to be consistent with your personal values, you will live a more fulfilling life. Your activities may be different if, for example, you value tranquility versus intensity or systemization versus spontaneity. What is important is that you are aware of and spend your time consistent with your values.

There is another perspective on the benefit of identifying and living to your values. In essence, your values are your legacy. Who you have become, in large part, is a result of the values you learned from your parents and grandparents. Similarly, think about the values you have passed along to your children and grandchildren. If you value integrity, so will they; if you value family, so will they; if you value faith, so will they. They will then pass along these values to subsequent generations. These values are your legacy.

There is no single right purpose or set of values for everyone. Rather, the answer to what are your life purpose and core values is what is right for you. It is best to look deeply within yourself to find that answer.

Live Accordingly

Elie Wiesel is a Holocaust survivor, Nobel Laureate, Andrew Mellon Professor of the Humanities at Boston University, peace activist, and author of 57 books. Wiesel says he is frequently asked by his BU students what they should most take away from his class, and he always gives them the same answer, "Regardless of what you pursue in your life, think higher and feel deeper."

Dan Price is an excellent example someone who thinks higher and feels deeper, and then lives accordingly.

In 1989, Dan attended a work-sponsored seminar that changed his life. The workshop was designed to teach Stephen Covey's *Seven Habits of Highly Effective People*. Also woven throughout the one-week event was an exercise to help Dan and the other attendees get in touch with their life purpose and core values. Importantly, the exercise included writing down what they learned about themselves. The purpose statement that Dan developed has guided him for over two-plus decades and is guiding him into his future.

Dan and Elise Price

Dan's purpose and values statement, which he calls "The Promise," begins, "My first priorities in life are my God and my family. This is evident from how I spend my time and live my life."

Dan's one-page typewritten purpose and values statement also includes these phrases:

"I will continue to be best friends and lovers with my Wife forever."

"My health is a blessing that I do not take for granted. I will use wisdom in what I eat, read, see, and do. I exercise my body and mind regularly."

"I see impossible situations as opportunities waiting to be discovered. I dare to be different."

"I listen twice as much as I speak. I hear both sides before judging. I am sincere and gentle, yet decisive. I live and lead by principles. I keep promises to others and myself. My word is my honor."

Dan refers to his retirement activities as "investments," making choices about how to spend his time based on "The Promise." Dan and his wife, Elise, are deeply involved in the lives of their children and of Dan's aging parents, who they support from several hours away, including Skyping frequently with his 87-year old mother. Dan is the Chairman of his church's Board of Elders, a position he also held before he retired. Dan and Elise are active in the church in other ways, including teaching the first grade Sunday school class together.

Dan has signed up to be a technical advisor for "Your Encore," a network of retired scientists and engineers that helps member companies increase the pace of their innovation. He envisions this role being helpful to his clients, but also to keep him stimulated mentally. Dan also attends to his physical well-being. In 2003, he attended another work-sponsored workshop that helped him learn more about exercise and nutrition. At the time, he weighed 210. He is now at 190 and still exercises regularly.

Mahatma Gandhi said, "The main purpose of life is to live rightly, think rightly, act rightly." Gandhi not only knew his life purpose, he relentlessly pursued it and he knew he was doing so. Dan Price, who has been retired for a year, knows who he is and lives accordingly.

Give it Your All

John Pepper's life purpose and core values have enabled him to live a full and fulfilling life both during and after his 40-year career with the Procter & Gamble Company, where he held the positions of President, Chief Executive Officer, and Chairman of the Board. Since moving on from P&G (John does not think about it as retiring, but rather as a new beginning to the next chapter of life), he has continued to pursue his life purpose—to be a positive influence on other people's lives just as others have influenced him. John's focus on others derives from his core belief that he is "here on earth for a reason."

John's new life chapter has been filled with family, friends, meaningful activities, and bringing his core values to companies and not-for-profit organizations. He was one of the early supporters of and, in 2006-7, was the Chief Executive Officer of Cincinnati's National Underground Railroad Freedom Center, where he continues to be involved. In addition to his work at the Freedom Center, over the past seven years, John has been Vice-President of Finance and Administration at Yale University, his alma mater; returned to the Board of Directors of Boston Scientific Corporation; and is currently Chairman of the Board of the Walt Disney Company.

John Pepper

Despite his career success, John has found that there is much more to life than financial security. John's happiness derives from being open to opportunities and becoming deeply involved in activities that are consistent with his purpose and values. He values family, serving others, continual learning and personal growth, wellness, doing meaningful things, and having fun. When asked how he chooses how to best spend his time, John said that he focuses on activities that help others while also helping him continually grow and be refreshed.

First on his priority list is spending more time with his wife, Francine, and their children and grandchildren than he had the opportunity to do while working. This has included bike-riding vacations with his sons and travel and visits with other family members. John also stays closely connected with a multitude of friends and former colleagues, keeping up with what and how they are doing. He is committed to a half-hour per day physical exercise regimen and finds every opportunity to continue to grow mentally by "keeping up with new things," like technology and subjects that attract his insatiable curiosity. In his spare time, John wrote *What Really Matters* (Yale University Press, 2007), a book whose title and text suggest that the fundamental question to be asked and answered in both business and personal life is the same.

While working at Yale, John was confronted with a major illness that served to reinforce many of the values of his life. His family rallied around him, providing the real-time support he needed. Prayers and well-wishes poured in from around the country and the world. John continued to work while receiving medical treatment, keeping a positive attitude that he would "beat this thing." He concentrated on those priorities that had a "forward focus" and that made the most difference to others. His philosophy to "give it your all; leaving no cards on the table" helped him through the illness and recovery.

John Pepper, among his many other skills, is a great teacher. He guides us to know our purpose and values; be open to opportunities that enable us to live by them; commit to serving others; gain joy from family and friends; continue to grow; have fun; and give it our all.

Key Learning about "Purpose/Values"

1. Individuals and organizations are more successful when they have a clear, compelling purpose and consistent personal values—and then live that way.
2. Purpose and values bring focus to your life and enable you to make choices consistent with what is important to you.
3. Many are not clear about their purpose or values, because they have never taken the time to think about them. Yet, through concentrated deliberation and discovery, you can uncover your purpose and values.

Getting Started

1. Seek to recall a point in time in your life where you had a crystal clear and compelling purpose. What was it and how did it make a difference to you and others?
2. If you do not have a written statement of your purpose and values, start by answering the following questions:
   a. You are 85 years old and your great grandchild, who is sitting on your lap, asks, "What has your life been about?" What would you say?

    b. From the list of values below (add others you think of), which are the top five that are most important in your life? Those you circle will be the values that you strive for every day.

3. Share your answers with close family members and friends who know you best to get their insights about you and your choices. Seek to learn from their experiences also.

Personal Values for you to consider:

Accomplishment	Freedom	Prosperity
Accountability	Friendship	Punctuality
Adventure	Fun	Quietude
Caring	Goodness	Reliability
Challenge	Gratitude	Resourcefulness
Change	Growth	Respect
Collaboration	Hard work	Responsiveness
Commitment	Honor	Rule of Law
Communication	Independence	Safety
Community	Individuality	Security
Competence	Innovation	Self-reliance
Competition	Integrity	Service
Connection	Intensity	Simplicity
Cooperation	Joy	Stability
Coordination	Justice	Standardization
Creativity	Knowledge	Status
Decisiveness	Love	Strength
Discipline	Loyalty	Success,
Discovery	Meaning	Teamwork
Diversity	Openness	Timeliness
Equality	Orderliness	Tolerance
Excellence	Patriotism	Tradition
Fairness	Peace	Tranquility
Faith	Perfection	Trust
Faithfulness	Pleasure	Truth
Family	Privacy	Wisdom

"Purpose/Values" Planning Worksheet

Personal Assessment: Rate the following statement from 1 to 5:
1 = This statement is far from describing my level of clarity.
5 = This statement fully describes my level of clarity.

"I am clear on my life purpose and core values."

Rating: 1   2   3   4   5

Planning for "Purpose/Values"

I am 85 years old and my great grandchild, who is sitting on your lap, asks, "What has your life been about?" What would I say?

_____

_____

_____

_____

_____

The top five values that are most important in my life:

1. _____

2. _____

3. _____

4. _____

5. _____

The one person in my life who can best help me to identify my Purpose and Values is _____

Start/Stop/Continue
Worksheet Instructions
For the Key Elements

You have been capturing your thoughts on worksheets provided earlier in the book. The worksheets in Chapters 8 through 15, however, are different, in that they introduce a new feature.

The difference is the addition of the Start/Stop/Continue approach, which is the basis of the planning you will be doing. The approach is simple, yet profound. You will determine there are activities that are missing in your life today, preventing you from achieving your goals. These are activities you will want to "Start" doing. There are activities you are doing today that are getting in the way of allowing you to achieve your goals; activities you will want to "Stop." There are also activities currently in your life that are fully consistent with meeting your life and retirement goals. These are activities you want to "Continue." Making choices about what to start, what to stop, and what to continue will be the essence of your planning.

Begin each worksheet by completing the assessment just as you have been doing on previous worksheets. Rate the assessment statement on the 1 to 5 scale. We cannot emphasize enough how important it is for you to be candid with yourself about your assessments. Your ratings are the basis upon which you will choose the activities that will change your life for the better. Only candid ratings will do you justice, and, remember, they are for "your eyes only."

The ratings are your indication of where you are in your life today, and you will be the best and final judge on how to turn the ratings into good choices. There are, however, some general guidelines for you to consider about how to best utilize the assessment ratings.

If you rate an assessment statement low (1 or 2), it indicates that you may either need to start activities to strengthen the key element or to stop activities that are holding you back. Using your knowledge about yourself, what you have learned in the chapter, what you can learn by talking to family and friends, and any other research you choose to do, write down those activities you decide to start or stop. A low rating does not preclude there being activities you choose to continue that may be working for you. These will not be your final lists; you will have other chances to decide which to do and when to do them as you complete your plan later. So, feel free to write down any activity you think might be applicable.

As an example, perhaps you decide in the "Well-Being" chapter that your rating is low because you do not have a regular and sufficient exercise program. Beginning such a program could be one of the activities you choose to start. Write it down. Or, perhaps your rating in "Fun" might be low, because there are activities that are draining a lot of your time without providing any pleasure or helping you in any other key element. These activities are taking the time you need to do other things more meaningful to you and might be on your stop list. Write them down.

If you rate an assessment statement high (4 or 5) for a key element, it indicates that what you are doing today is right for you—there may be activities in your life you will want to highlight to make sure you continue them. Take time to think about what these might be; you may have been doing them for so long that you are not aware of what is actually working for you. Writing down these key activities will validate them and make sure you do not get complacent about this key element being a strength in your life.

For example, you might rate "Connectedness" high in part because your extended family gets together every Sunday after church. You may want to continue this activity. Write it down. Or, perhaps you rate Financial Security high, in part, because you have engaged a financial advisor and are tracking your expenses and regularly comparing them to your budget. You may want to continue these activities. Write them down.

A higher rating does not preclude their being activities you choose to start and stop that may be missing in your live or getting in your way, respectively.

If you assess a key element in the middle (3), there may be a balance of items you want to start, stop, and continue, or this could indicate you might want to focus your efforts on higher priority areas, at least in the near term. Regardless, think about the key element and the possible start, stop, and continue choices. Write them down.

The assessments and indicated actions are only guidelines to prompt you to think about your individual situation. Initially, list all of those activities (using extra paper if needed) that you believe fit the start/stop/continue choices. Think about this as brainstorming to help ensure you create a robust list. Remember, you will have an opportunity to come back later to make choices and set priorities.

Research and our experience show that unless you act upon a new insight within 24 hours of learning it and try to practice it for at least 21 days, it is unlikely you will make the sustained change in your life you want to make. We discussed this in Chapter 1, "Get Serious about Your Retirement," and will cover this in more depth in Chapter 18, "Doing What You Planned." For now, circle those one or two activities that you will likely want to act on immediately, once your full plan is established later in the book. Again, you are not yet committing to yourself to do these; you are merely beginning to move toward action on those items you eventually choose to do.

You will probably generate some additional insights as you think through your action lists. Write these in the "Other thoughts" section of the worksheets.

Finally, the best known approach indicates that it is important to have someone who can work with you to support your change. The best person to support you will not necessarily be the same person for each key element. For each element, select someone who has your best interests at heart, will be candid with you, and will hold you accountable. Think critically about who he or she might be for each and write the name at the bottom of the worksheet; you will use these names later.

As a reminder, we suggest that you complete each worksheet when you get to it. You will eventually use the collection of all the worksheets to develop your unique personal retirement plan.

Chapter 8

Attitude

"Attitude is a little thing that makes a big difference."
Winston Churchill

"Whether you think you can or you think you can't, you're right."
Henry Ford

Do You Know?

Those with a positive attitude live almost eight years longer on average and are significantly less likely to become frail as they age.

Attitude significantly influences the quality of your relationships, how you think about your financial security, and how you respond to health-related issues—all of which are critical to a fulfilling retirement.

What is "Attitude?"

In 1979, Ellen Langer, a professor at the Harvard Business School, reconfigured a monastery to look as if it were 1959. Everything was changed (e.g. magazines, newspapers, TV shows, pictures on the walls, and even conversations) to reflect that time two decades earlier. A group of elderly men in their 70s and early 80s from a local nursing home were asked to live there for a week. Even the photo IDs they were given when they arrived represented an earlier life. They lived as though 1959 were the present.

The results were astonishing. In only a week, signs of aging reversed themselves. The men looked and acted younger; their joints were more flexible; their posture had straightened; and they actually lost body fat. When Langer changed the men's environment, she altered their mindset about how old they were. The attitude change then affected their physical well-being.

Attitude can affect your perception of everything from financial security to how you approach your relationships with others; from your ability to have fun to how you approach life in general. You know people who have optimistic, positive, hopeful, engaging attitudes and those who are quite the opposite. Which of these people would you rather be in a room with?

Parents, marketers, teachers, political activists, despots, and others have successfully used persuasion to change the attitudes of children, consumers, students, citizens, individuals, and the masses. We all know of personal stories, as well as historical references, when attitudes have been changed—sometimes for the good and sometimes not.

Over the last decade, "positive psychology" has become a much researched and touted branch of the science. It is focused on how individuals "...derive a positive sense of well-being, belonging, meaning, and purpose..." Positive psychology is learning what many have known intuitively, that we have the capacity to persuade ourselves to have the attitude necessary to make a positive difference in our own lives.

For but one of many examples, financial security is, in some ways, a function of our perception and attitude. There are those who have millions in their portfolio who do not feel they have enough and are unhappy. There are those who have modest funds, yet feel the funds are fully sufficient and they are happy. You will see the concept of attitude permeating each of the key elements of a fulfilling retirement.

There is a video that has made the rounds on the internet that may be the very definition of attitude. Fran, who had just turned 90, and Marlo Cowan have been married for 62 years. They are seen in the video in the atrium of the Mayo Clinic. In the atrium is a piano. The couple stands in front of the keys; leans into the piano; and, without sitting, begins to play a honky-tonk duet rendition of "Old Grey Bonnet." She starts on the low keys and he on the high keys. About 45 seconds into the tune, smiling and even giggling all the while, they change places on the keyboard, not skipping a beat. As he passes her while making the switch, he playfully pats her behind. By now, a crowd has assembled and is laughing along with the couple. A few seconds later, they switch again; this time she pats *his* behind. On the next switch, he goes to pat her behind, but her hands meet his and they pat hands, again, not skipping a beat. They end the tune, the assembled crowd breaks into applause, the couple smiles and walks off.

One minute and 14 seconds with the Cowans demonstrates many important aspects of retirement—having the attitude to keep themselves and others upbeat; having fun as evidenced by their smiles and giggles; and enjoying a special relationship. They bubble with positive energy, and, given that energy is contagious, it spills over to others, including those who watch the video, who cannot help but to also have fun.

Satchel Paige, perhaps the greatest Negro League and, arguably, the greatest any-league pitcher in baseball history, was once asked his age—a statistic that was frequently debated. Satch, who was a major league rookie in his early 40s and pitched for the Kansas City Athletics at age 60, answered the question, saying less about his age than about his general philosophy of life. He responded with a much more profound question of his own, "How old would you be if you didn't know how old you was?"

Paige routinely and inadvertently (or perhaps not) espoused life philosophy when talking about baseball. A stretch of the imagination makes Satchel Paige the patron saint of the retiree. Try these on for size.

"Age is a question of mind over matter. If you don't mind, it doesn't matter."

"I never had a job. I always played baseball."

"You win a few, you lose a few. Some get rained out. But you got to dress for all of them."

"Don't look back. Something might be gaining on you."

Satchel Paige looked toward the future with anticipation and was always ready to play; he approached baseball as a passion, not as a job; and he decided that age was not an issue for him. Why? Because he instinctively knew that there is freedom in believing that age "doesn't matter."

Having a positive attitude in retirement is not just about thinking young, but it does help. Ellen Langer, Fran and Marlo Cowan and Satchel Paige taught us that in many ways, life is about positive attitude—and about deciding to have one.

Secret 6: Mindset
- Retirement is a state of mind—if you think you are old, you will be.
- Have a positive mindset and think and act as if you did not know how old you are—it will permeate every other aspect of your retirement.

Your Attitude is Everything

Attitude is complex and subjective. One definition is, "a complex mental state involving beliefs and feelings and values and dispositions to act in certain ways." Despite its complexity, attitude is one of those things in the category of "you'll know it when you see it," both in yourself and in others.

There are two relevant questions: 1) Is there value in controlling attitude? 2) If there is, can you do so? The question of should you control your attitude has been thoroughly researched and the definitive answer is "yes." Having a positive attitude can have a meaningful effect on your longevity and well-being.

The Ohio Longitudinal Study of Aging and Retirement, led by Becca Levy, Ph.D. and others from Yale University, is a 20-plus-year trial that examined, among other things, the attitudes of people 50 and over toward aging. Two of the study's findings: 1) people with a positive attitude about growing older lived an average of 7.5 years longer than those with a negative attitude; and 2) those with more positive attitudes reported better functional health.

The University of California-San Diego School of Medicine conducted a study of 500 representative older Americans between the ages of 60 and 98. The key result of the study was summarized by researcher Dilip Jeste, "What is most interesting about this study is that people who think they are aging well are not necessarily the most healthy individuals. In fact, optimism and effective coping styles were found to be more important to aging successfully than traditional measures of health and wellness. These findings suggest that physical health is not the best indicator of successful aging - attitude is."

In a study of over 1500 older people in the Mexican-American community, the University of Texas investigated the relationship between attitude and frailty. At the beginning of the seven-year study, all of the study participants were in relatively good health. The researchers measured the development of frailty using weight loss, exhaustion levels, walking speed, and grip strength. They found those people who had a positive attitude towards life were significantly less likely to become frail.

These are but some of the research examples that have found and confirmed that a positive attitude has a measurable effect on longevity and quality of life as we age. You should, therefore, be concerned about our attitude and, by inference, should we make an effort to make and keep it positive.

The question of how to control our attitude to make it more positive is more difficult. There are numerous resources, such as books, articles, and web sites, to help you find ways to improve your attitude. One such book is *Fire Up Your Life Now! 25 Secrets for Creating the Life You Really Want* by Allan and Barbara Kenyon.

The Kenyons are both personal and business coaches, who have learned the importance of attitude from their many years of helping clients. In the book, they share their 25 secrets, most of which are focused on various aspects of modifying attitude. They provide insights and exercises to help the reader reflect on his or her own situation and what changes could be made.

Among their secrets are "Fear is Not to be Feared," "Say Good-Bye to Self-doubt," "Persistence Wins," and, most explicitly, "Your Attitude is Everything."

Attitude is important to your success in retirement life, and you can positively affect it.

You Can't Afford to be Tired

(Alan Spector) While I was still working, there was a period when my part of the business was going through a particularly difficult time. We were faced with significant business problems, and my work group had some difficult personnel issues.

I was in a meeting at 6:30pm, having been at work since 6:00 that morning. Our leadership team had convened to review how our latest plans were progressing and where our remaining problems were. Although our team had worked together for some time and were very supportive of each other, nerves were frayed because of the current situation—we had all been doing 14-hour days for a couple of weeks.

Each of us shared our progress, problems, and plans. When it was my turn, I reviewed both the business actions I had taken and the status of my personnel issues, which had the potential of exacerbating the business situation. When I completed my review, which included answering some tough but fair questions from my colleagues, our Human Resources team member, Gail Prather, proceeded to give me a list of additional things she thought I needed to do to resolve my workgroup personnel problems.

I bluntly responded that I did not plan to act on any of her suggestions. She asked why not.

"Because I'm tired," I responded.

Her comeback put me over the edge. She said, "You can't afford to be tired."

I did something way out of character for me. I dropped the "F-bomb" on her and walked out of the room. I had never done anything like that before, nor have I done anything like that since, neither in business nor personal life.

I did not even go to my office. I just left the building, went to my car, and drove home. During the 15-minute ride, I had time to reflect on the overall situation and my less-than-businesslike behavior. It finally struck me what she was trying to tell me, and she was right.

Tired is a state-of-mind. Sure, I was mentally drained, sleep-deprived, and, like my colleagues, on edge. But, I had it in my power to merely decide not to be tired, or, at least, not to let being tired negatively affect me. I learned a lot about myself that day and a lot about attitude. That evening, I decided to not be tired; at least, not so tired as to act the way I did.

The following morning, I went straight to Gail's office. She had a knowing smile on her face. Somehow she anticipated my self-reflection and my attitude adjustment. I apologized to her, thanked her for her insight, and asked her to repeat her personnel suggestions. We discussed them and I decided to implement several of them. Not surprisingly, they were successful.

Through continued hard work, teamwork, and a little luck, we resolved our business issues, and I solved my personnel problems. Those difficult times made a big difference in my life, as did Gail Prather.

Whenever I get close to needing an attitude adjustment about anything, I think of that incident and of Gail. She was right and still is. When it comes to attitude, I can just decide to adjust it.

No Big Deal

The senior baseball community is made up of older players, many in their 40s, 50s, 60s, and beyond. Senior baseball players are a great source of examples of how attitude can make a positive difference in a person's life.

These seniors are still playing baseball, because they are still passionate about the game and nostalgic about how they loved it when they were younger. There is a saying in the senior baseball community, "You don't stop playing because you are growing old; you stop growing old because you are playing."

In 2002, Jerry Wuest attended a Cincinnati Reds Baseball Heaven fantasy camp. At the time, he was 63 and had contracted Parkinson's disease. When off the field, he used a cane and frequently had difficulty taking a first step to begin walking. It was not uncommon for him to fall and wait good-naturedly for help to get up. Yet, during camp, Jerry always took his turn at bat, albeit being assigned a pinch runner. During each at bat, he would hit the ball, which he did frequently and squarely, and with absolutely no hesitation or indication of his illness, would take off from the batter's box for a few steps toward first base as the pinch runner took over.

During one at bat, Jerry did not stop after a few steps. His baseball instincts overcame his infirmity. He put his head down and he ran all the way to first base. There was no doubt at the end of the week who his team's Most Valuable Player selection would be. Jerry's attitude and love of the game inspired everyone throughout the week and beyond.

Tom Cretella, in his early 60s, is another example of how attitude can make a difference. Tom runs and walks with a limp because he has an artificial hip. Yet he still is a catcher and first baseman and has a formidable on-base percentage. When not playing baseball, Tom is a serious hiker with a special interest in steep-hill climbing.

Dick Irvin is a 75-year-old player from St. George, Utah. Dick was once asked if he had ever had any injuries that had kept him from playing senior baseball. His response not only said a lot about him but also captured the spirit of senior baseball players who truly believe they are never too old to play. Dick said, "I have a replaced hip and at times it gives me trouble. Many other bumps and strains that come along. No big deal."

Perhaps the best senior baseball example of attitude overcoming age and making a positive difference in the life of the individual and those around him is George Goodall. In mid-2002, George Goodall got on a plane in St. Louis, nearby his home in Belleville, Illinois, and traveled, by himself, to Beijing, China to play baseball.

For the next week, George kept up with all of the sightseeing and played in games against Chinese locals with other Americans who had made the trip. The average age of the American players and the spouses who made the trip was about 45. This calculation included George, whose 60-year old glove was older than virtually every player on either the American or Chinese teams. George was 92 at the time.

When he came up for his first at-bat against a Chinese team, the fielders put down their gloves and applauded George Goodall, en masse. The Chinese revere their elders, the Chinese team loved baseball, and they respected George's attitude. It was an inspirational moment.

George Goodall in China at age 92

George Goodall had the attitude that enabled him to envision making the trip, continue to play ball, and energetically tell great stories to anyone who wanted to listen, and there were many who gathered around to do just that. His attitude also allowed him to display a baseball in his home upon which was simply printed, "Played ball on the Great Wall of China, 14 May 02."

Jerry, Tom, Dick, and George each illustrate an attitude that enabled them to pursue a passion, overcome aging and medical issues, have fun, and live the life they wanted.

Key Learning about "Attitude"

1. A positive attitude can add to your longevity and quality of life.
2. Attitude is a foundation block to a fulfilling retirement, because it can affect so many aspects of your life.
3. Making the choice to have a positive attitude is one of the many cost-free things you can do to enhance your retirement.

Getting Started

1. Begin and end your day by expressing gratitude for all that is right in your life. For example, as you get up in the morning and go to bed at night, think of three things you are blessed with, not repeating the same ones you said the last time. Appreciate the many "magic moments" you have in your life every day.
2. Surround yourself with a positive environment. While you may not always be successful at doing so, identify and eliminate those things that can darken your day, such as the evening news, people who are negative, rush hour traffic—anything that dampens your bright outlook and experience of the day. "Unplug" from whatever depletes you.
3. Think young. Ask yourself, as did Satchel Paige, "How old would you be if you didn't know how old you was?" Mentally teleport yourself back 20 years and see what happens.
4. Have positive dialogues with yourself. Many of your thoughts may be negative, such as lamenting how old you are or how the past was so much better. Do not get caught up in "thought attacks." Be aware of this "self talk," and choose to think of the present and what is good.
5. Take responsibility for your life. Many people point to others to explain their circumstances, placing blame and increasing negativity over time. Think "I will personally determine the quality of my retirement." This attitude will enable you to fully enjoy all the freedom and fun that this time of life has to offer.

"Attitude" Planning Worksheet

Personal Assessment: Rate the following statement from 1 to 5:
1 = This statement is far from describing my attitude.
5 = This statement fully describes my attitude.

"Those closest to me describe me as having a positive attitude."

Rating: 1   2   3   4   5

Planning for "Attitude"
What I will CONTINUE to do:

_____

_____

What I will START doing:

_____

_____

What I will STOP doing:

_____

_____

Other thoughts about Attitude:

_____

_____

The one person in my life who can best help me to implement my immediate next step regarding Attitude is

_____

Chapter 9

Well-Being

"Failure is more frequently from want of energy than want of capital."
Daniel Webster

"And what is a man without energy?
Nothing – nothing at all."
Mark Twain

Do You Know?

Beginning at age 30, you lose 2% of your capacity (energy) to live life, unless you take steps to offset the loss.

One in five Americans becomes sufficiently disabled by their 60s to affect their daily activities; despite many of the disabilities being preventable.

Ninety percent of Americans get less than 30 minutes of exercise per day; well below recommendations to minimize risk of heart disease, cancer, and other illnesses.

Weighing the same at age 55 as you did when you were 18 reduces the risk of serious disease by 80%.

Only about 30% of well-being and longevity is dictated by genetics—the remainder is a function of personal daily habits and environment.

About half of us will die prematurely and by an average of 12 years.

Those who attend to their well-being are 14 times more likely to survive major surgery; are at a 20% lower risk of heart disease; will have a slower progression of dementia; will experience a higher level of marital stability; and have a greater measure of life satisfaction.

What is "Well-Being?"

There are many ways to think about well-being, and, fortunately, they all have the same indicated actions. We have found it is most compelling to think about well-being as having extraordinary energy to live a full and fulfilling retirement life. Consider all of the things you may want to do in retirement. Regardless of what they are, you will need to have the energy to do them now and into your future. There are only so many hours in a day; should you not have the energy to make the best use of each one?

The key to gaining and sustaining energy is developing deliberate habits across each of the four dimensions of energy: Physical, Emotional, Mental, and Purpose.

Physical Energy is about the quantity of energy you have and is influenced by your exercise, nutrition, breathing, and recovery habits. When you get these behaviors right, your capacity to do things will increase and enable you to stay active throughout each day and over the years. Here are some questions to ask yourself about your Physical Energy:

- Do you do sufficient aerobic exercise (enough to break a sweat) for at least 30 minutes three days a week?
- Do you do exercises every day to stretch and remain flexible?
- Do you do some kind of resistance training (like lift weights) at least twice per week?
- Do you get up and move around every 90 minutes to keep your energy flowing?
- Do you eat light, often, and nutritiously?
- Do you consume smart low-glycemic snacks?
- Do you get seven to eight hours of restful sleep each night? Do you take an occasional short nap when you need one?
- Do you take time to fully get away (like vacations with no electronic connections) to recharge your batteries?

Emotional Energy is the quality of your energy and is affected by how you think and feel. When you are at high levels of positive emotional energy, you are engaged, focused, challenged, optimistic, confident, and calm. You will not be experiencing frustration, anger, fear, resentment, impatience, or sadness. These negative emotions drain energy and, if they persist, can become sources of illness. There are things you can do to maximize positive emotional energy and minimize the negative. You learned more about generating positive emotional energy in the last chapter about "Attitude." Some questions about your Emotional Energy:

- Do you appreciate and are you grateful for what you have in your life today?
- Do you focus on what is positive?
- Are you cool under stress?
- Do you surround yourself with a positive environment (people, music, etc.) and get rid of the "energy vampires?"
- Are you respectful and appreciative of others? For example, do you say, "Please" and "Thank you."

Mental Energy is about keeping your mind sharp and focused. You can assess your level of mental energy by considering how well you can and do focus on the task at hand and how well you manage distractions. The chapter about "Growth" will give you more insights regarding mental energy. Some questions about your Mental Energy:

- Do you envision daily what success looks like?
- Do you focus on what you can directly influence?
- Do you shake up your routine; even in small ways (e.g., taking a different way home from the store)?
- Do you stimulate yourself intellectually to remain sharp (e.g., doing a crossword puzzle every day, taking a class)?
- Do you seek opportunities to learn new skills (e.g., cooking, dancing)?

Purpose is your source of motivation, determination, and endurance. It provides direction to focus your energy in the right direction. Purpose is pursuing your reason for being and being part of something greater than yourself. The chapter about "Purpose and Values" spoke to the importance of your commitment to life purpose and core values, which will lift your energy of purpose. Some questions about your Purpose Energy:

- Are you clear about what you are seeking to do with your life?
- Can you explain to others what is truly important to you; your deeply held values?
- Are you certain which roles you play in life are most important to you?
- Do you have a list of dreams you want to pursue?
- Do you care deeply about something beyond yourself?

As you build your personal energy across each of the four dimensions, you will be more creative, productive, and collaborative; be less prone to illness; have higher levels of retention; and live a longer, happier life. Also, since energy is contagious, others will enjoy being around you, as you will be a Tigger in their lives as opposed to an Eyore (if you are not familiar with the *Winnie the Pooh* stories, look into the relative energy levels of Tigger and Eyore).

The good news is that one of the benefits of retirement is that you will have more time to focus on each of the energy dimensions. Said bluntly, the excuse of not having the time for an exercise program because of all of the hours spent at work or building a family no longer applies. The excuse that it is difficult to maintain proper nutrition when eating in work cafeterias or on business trips no longer applies. The excuse that you cannot take the time to take the steps to relieve unnecessary stress no longer applies. The excuse that you do not have the time to get a proper night's sleep no longer applies. Start and continue energy building behaviors, and stop energy draining behaviors.

While we are choosing to focus on energy as a path to well-being, we would be remiss if we did not say something about well-being as the absence of illness. Proper exercise, nutrition, breathing, and recovery behaviors will take you a long way toward avoiding illness, but they complement, not substitute for good preventative medicine. Early detection and treatment of illness is critical to your well-being. Checkups such as annual physicals and eye exams, semi-annual dentist visits, other recommended periodic tests, and seeing the right medical professional when symptoms arise are all a part of maintaining and growing your physical energy; as are daily hygiene habits, like tooth brushing, flossing, and frequent hand washing. If any of these or similar checkups or habits are not part of your routine, it behooves you to include them in your plan as an activity to start. Do what you can to take a preventative approach. Illness drains energy.

Role Model

Neither we nor you are naïve about illness. There are health conditions that can significantly and negatively affect your ability to enjoy a perfectly fulfilling retirement. That being said, it is our contention that if you build and sustain your energy level, even in the face of illness, your ability to deal with the illness will be greatly enhanced.

Harvey Ferdman is passionate about computer technology and was fortunate to put himself in a position to pursue it as a career. He studied computer science in college before there were such degrees and became a systems engineer, the technical member of his company's systems and software sales team. Over his career, Harvey also held sales positions, but always gravitated back to the technology.

That was until May 2003, when Harvey, at age 50, was diagnosed with colon cancer, which needed to be treated very aggressively and immediately. He underwent 30 days of radiation and chemotherapy, had major surgery, and returned for another six months of intense chemotherapy. From the perspective of the battle with the cancer itself, the treatment was successful; Harvey's current cancer status is referred to as "no evidence detected."

Harvey Ferdman

Accompanying the good news about the success are also a number of residual effects from the cancer, the surgeries, and the treatments that take a great deal of time and attention to manage on a daily basis. As a result, Harvey has not been able to work and is officially on medical retirement.

Many with similar conditions become inactive and isolated—not so for Harvey. He has been determined to remain active, engaged, insatiably curious, and involved with his family, friends, and causes. How does he do this? Harvey is a role model for building and sustaining energy, attending to each of its four dimensions.

Harvey builds physical energy by primarily focusing on his nutrition and practicing Qigong, a Chinese practice that uses slow movements and controlled breathing to enhance circulation, flexibility, and overall health. Qigong also helps Harvey with his emotional and mental energy as it is a meditative practice that induces personal serenity.

Harvey studies and eats a balanced and organic diet. He has been a shareholder in two organic farms and active in the community gardening movement. This past year, with help from his daughter, Julie, he built and planted an extensive organic garden in his backyard.

Qigong is not the only activity that Harvey pursues to build emotional energy. He spends as much time as possible with immediate and extended family, drawing unbounded energy from his precocious three-year old granddaughter, Luna. Another example is his involvement in colon cancer support groups. During his cancer treatment, Harvey found little readily-available information and a lack of support groups for his type of cancer. He advocated for starting a group and continues to be involved as a mentor for those who have been recently diagnosed. Harvey inspires others and is emotionally enriched by the interaction, especially and frequently when he receives a heartfelt thank you for the help he provides.

Harvey has always had an insatiable curiosity. It is this curiosity that enables him to build mental energy. Despite no longer working in the computer business, he stays up to date with the latest technology, frequently being the first one to own the newest advancement. He not only enjoys the features of each device, but seeks to understand the inner workings. His interest in knowledge goes beyond technology, however, as Harvey studies everything from political issues, to food nutrition and healthy cooking, to learning about Eastern medicine, to innumerable other topics. If he has a question, he will not stop until he knows the answer.

Harvey views himself as a citizen of the world; a part of

something greater than himself. He remains committed to, acts upon, and, importantly, draws energy of purpose from the Jewish concept of "tikkun olam," which speaks to the human responsibility of repairing what is wrong in the world. He readily volunteers to help others, gets involved with causes and candidates; and is the first to lend support to a family member in need.

Harvey's absolute health is less than ideal, and his medical issues do, in reality, limit what he can do. Harvey's high energy level, however, enables him to live fully every day.

Practice What I Preach

(Keith Lawrence) I struggled to maintain a healthy body weight early in my life. When I was ten years old, I had a serious foot injury and was laid up an entire summer. My weight ballooned and I was heavy into my high school years. It was then that my good friend, Mike Neuhaus, helped me get down to a fit 175 pounds. Mike and I rode our bicycles everywhere and played tennis every chance we got. I felt great physically and was proud of myself.

I maintained my weight through college, because I continued good habits. When I graduated, I began working at Procter & Gamble's largest manufacturing plant. It was a great career opportunity, but my work schedule really messed up the healthy habits I had formed. The plant operated on a swing shift, which meant that I rotated through a schedule of third shift to second shift to first shift every month—each rotation lasting seven days. I was unable to get into good sleep or eating patterns, and I soon found my weight at 220 pounds.

Two things happened that enabled me to regain my fitness. One was that I moved to a work assignment that was not on a swing shift. The other was my wife and children. I decided that if I were going to be a great father and, eventually, grandfather, I would need to be healthy and fit. I began a regimen of exercise and nutrition. When I moved to Cincinnati, a new friend, Mike Ferrari, became my gym partner, helping me hold myself accountable for sticking to my new good habits. I returned to my high school weight and have maintained it over the years. I feel as good today as I did at 30. Having someone who cares about you and helps you hold yourself accountable to live the habits of energy management is absolutely essential.

Several years ago, I had the opportunity to attend a work-sponsored training seminar that introduced me to the concept of multi-dimensional energy development. The training reinforced my exercise and nutrition habits, and it taught me about other ways to improve my overall energy—helping me focus on the emotional, mental, and purpose components to complement my physical fitness. I was so influenced by the training, I offered to become a trainer and have shared it with thousands of people around the world. Becoming a trainer has helped me be disciplined to "practice what I preach." As I teach this course, I seek to learn from others' experiences to give me new ideas to try out and improve what I do to remain fit and full of vibrant energy. It also enables me to live my purpose of "enabling dreams" by helping others improve their well-being.

Super-Size Guy

Dr. Richard Gimpelson is a gynecologist who has experienced both ends of the well-being scale. Before July 2003, even though he knew better, Richard carried 285 pounds on a short frame and characterized his lifestyle as "...years of abuse replete with milkshakes, hamburgers, French fries, and hot-fudge sundaes. I was a 'super-size' guy. I'd super-size orders for myself and my wife just so I could eat hers too. All my life, I was a quantity eater, not a quality eater. I could eat 30 White Castles or an entire pizza—no problem."

After July 2003, Richard lost nearly 100 pounds on an 1800-calorie per day diet and began to exercise regularly. He appropriately started his exercise program slowly but now says, "If I don't work out at least four days a week, I'll feel guilty. I'll even park my car far away from my building and walk the stairs instead of taking the elevator—any excuse to do a little more."

What is the significance of July 2003? It was a heart attack and a prognosis from his cardiologist. Richard describes what the cardiologist said, "He told me, 'You've had a heart attack. You have to exercise, lose weight, and change your diet, or you will die.' I think I needed that; if he had said, 'You might die,' I would have gone on the same way I had been."

Richard learned his lesson and shares his story with anyone who will listen. He teaches us that we have the opportunity to make behavior changes before getting into trouble. As Richard, now in his mid 60s, begins thinking about retirement, he can do so from a platform of being physically fit, organically well, and filled with energy.

Jenny

Ed Friedman is a 63-year old accountant and certified "QuickBooks Pro Advisor." Ed grew up in an observant Jewish home, then drifted away from orthodoxy when he was married at age 21. When his marriage unraveled 20 years later and he lost all of his tangible possessions, Ed began to search for something on a spiritual level. He returned to his observant roots, but still did not feel as though he had fully reconnected with his faith.

In 2003, his daughter, Jenny, died from complications resulting from congenital heart issues. Self-reflection following Jenny's death moved Ed toward a higher spiritual level and prompted him to begin studying the Talmud, the record of rabbinic discussions pertaining to Jewish law. His is not a minor commitment. Ed is part of a study group called "Daf Yomi," which means "a page a day." He studies every evening and is more than halfway through the seven years it will take to complete "the cycle," studying each of the 2711 pages of the Talmud. What happens when Ed completes "the cycle?" He will start all over again. Ed looks forward to studying every evening after work and plans to continue into retirement. "Every night I can't wait to learn what the Talmud will say."

Ed Friedman is building his emotional and mental energy along with his energy of purpose. He is also pursuing a passion and getting a head start on an activity he will continue into retirement.

Key Learning about "Well-Being"

1. You need to take positive action to maintain your capacity to live to the fullest.
2. Being well is not only being free of illness, but also having sufficient energy to live the life you want, now and into your future.

3. A deliberate choice of the right daily habits will grow your energy and your capacity to deal with the demands of the fulfilling retirement you want. These habits can have a positive impact on both your longevity and the quality of your life.
4. The demands of building families and careers provide us with "excuses" for not having the time to build good habits of well-being. Once you retire, there should be no excuse for bad well-being habits.

Getting Started

1. Gain insight about the relationship between your age and your daily habits:
   a. www.BlueZones.com (Vitality Compass)
   b. www.RealAge.com (RealAge Test).
2. Choose one new well-being habit to begin practicing now for the next 21 days and get a partner to do it with you to help hold yourself accountable. An example might be taking a brisk 30-minute walk three or more times per week. This investment will help you gain more energy now and will encourage you to successfully add other habits.
3. Each day, assess what energizes you and what drains you. Make choices to do more of what adds energy to your life and move away from the things and people that deplete you.

"Well-Being" Planning Worksheet

Personal Assessment: Rate the following statement from 1 to 5:
1 = This statement in no way describes my state of energy and well-being.
5 = This statement fully describes my state of energy and well-being.

"I have sufficient energy to fully do what I want to do in my life. I will be able to sustain this well into my retirement."

      Rating: 1   2   3   4   5

Planning for "Well-Being"

What I will CONTINUE to do:

_____

_____

What I will START doing:

_____

_____

What I will STOP doing:

_____

_____

Other thoughts about Well-Being:

_____

_____

The one person in my life who can best help me to implement my immediate next step regarding Well-Being is

_____

Chapter 10

Financial Security

"I am opposed to millionaires,
but it would be dangerous to offer me the position."
Mark Twain

"It's easy to have principles when you're rich.
The important thing is to have principles
when you're poor."
Ray Kroc

> # Do You Know?
>
> Only 35% of pre-retirees have a written plan for their future finances.
>
> A key to financial security is living below your means, matching your lifestyle choices to your level of resources.
>
> Regardless of the size of your nest egg, a measure of financial security is whether you are worrying about your money.
>
> Sixty-one percent of retirees spend more than expected on health care, thereby putting a dent in their financial plans.

What is "Financial Security?"

While we believe and the gist of the book is that retirement success is not all about the money, we also know that financial security is an important element of a fulfilling retirement. And, you will recall, the first question we suggest you ask and answer to determine if it is time for you to retire is, "Do you have enough?"

Many future and current retirees believe that financial security and, for that matter, retirement happiness are based solely on having a lot of money. Financial security and having a lot of money are not the same things. Financial security is matching your lifestyle to your level of financial resources and can be measured by whether you are worried about your finances.

It is not our intent to create a primer on how you should manage your money. There are many great books, web-based resources, and financial advisors to help. Rather, our intent is to provide you with a framework to guide your thinking about this important aspect. The list below is what we believe can help lead you to achieve the financial security you seek. We do not view the list as a menu from which to choose one or two items, but rather as items that all need to be addressed.

One last time—this list is about achieving financial security, not about making a lot of money.

1. Match your lifestyle to whatever level of resources you have. There are successes and failures in every economic bracket; for example, those with modest funds who have successfully and happily matched their lives to their resources and those with significant funds who have outspent their resources or are always worried about their money. Here are several steps to achieve this aspect of financial security:

   a. Understand what your resources really are. You may be able to do this yourself, or you may want to take advantage of a trusted professional or someone in your family or a friend who is knowledgeable.

   b. Understand what you are spending and project what you will spend in retirement. The best way to do this is to track how much you are spending and on what, creating the specificity of line items you need to help you make good decisions.

   c. Create a budget that allows you to live below your means, and then continue to track your spending to ensure you are meeting your budget. Some people like and are comfortable with complex spreadsheets; others are not. You can make your tracking system as simple as creating a checking account in which you deposit what you want to spend each month, pay all of your bills out of that account, and track how many months you are at or below your target. Or you can create a "line-item" spreadsheet—whichever works best for you. If you keep track of how you are doing versus your budget, you will be able to quickly identify when you are overspending and can investigate to figure out why.

   d. Create a systematic withdrawal of funds to replace your paycheck and to create a rhythm of income and spending. Said simply, transfer the right amount of money (taking into account your level of resources, spending level, tax implications, et al.) from your retirement funds into your checking account on a monthly basis. It is like paying yourself as if retirement is your job.

2. Put a solid foundation in place to help you deal with inevitable financial bumps in the road. The foundation is built on three components:

    a. Have a written financial plan. Both creating the plan and writing it down will help you think through your options and get very specific about what you want to do.

    b. If you have a spouse or partner, work on and agree to your plan with him or her. The last thing you want to do is start having the conversation about your situation for the first time when a crisis arises.

    c. Reach out to experts; you spent the first half of your life in school and in your career learning from teachers, masters, and mentors to improve your knowledge and skills. Trying to "go-it-alone" as you develop your financial future is counter to what made you successful all of your life. The experts can help you keep the emotion out of your decision making; even good financial advisors have financial advisors to help manage their funds and financial decisions. This does not mean you should turn your finances over to someone without staying closely involved and monitoring their activities. It is your personal responsibility. Follow the advice of President Reagan, airline pilots, and others, "Trust, but verify." Another way to think about this is for you to become an "informed delegator," having the experts use their knowledge and skills on your behalf, but staying informed of their actions. Importantly, find someone who you personally trust and whose values and perspectives align most closely with yours (e.g., overall risk tolerance and sense of optimism about the economy).

3. Take steps to reduce your risk of having potential circumstances negatively affect your financial situation. For example:

    a. Talk to your aging parents and ask them to share their financial situation with you, so that you can help them manage it as they become less able to do so, including finding out if they will need financial support from you.

    b. Talk to your children to let them know you are living within your means and you want them to do the same. Let them know, if it is appropriate for you, to expect you to provide a short-term financial safety net when they have difficulties, but not if they are frivolous about their finances and their planning.

4. Have a financial plan that goes beyond managing your money in the near term. For example, develop an estate plan and an insurance portfolio that best meet your needs and protect you and your family into the future.

5. Recognize that financial security has a lot to do with your perception of it and your attitude toward it. If you have taken the steps noted above and have developed a holistic retirement plan by using this book, you can consider yourself financially secure, regardless of your economic level. Dan Kiley, President of The Retirement Corporation of America and founder of Retirement University, addresses this point when he says, "True financial security is freedom, and if you're worried about your money, you are not financially secure, regardless of how much money you have."

The answer, therefore, to what is financial security is both what you make of it and what you think of it. Financial security is not a given level of assets. It is taking the steps that enable you to focus on the non-financial aspects of life to allow you to create a fulfilling retirement.

Achieving Financial Insecurity

Throughout the book, we are sharing stories of people who have experiences relevant to the subject matter at hand. We do this because personal stories can help you better relate to how each chapter can impact your future. In the case of each of the stories, the people are real and are happy to be sharing their experiences with you. In this chapter, we are sharing the stories of real people, but are not using their real names because we chose not to put people in that position in association with financial information. These financial security stories, therefore, will be told with fictitious first names. This first set of vignettes speaks to the importance of financial planning and taking the time to understand the implications of your decisions.

Bob was offered a retirement package by his employer and jumped at the chance to live out his lifelong dream, sailing around the world. At first blush, that sounds exciting and an opportunity to pursue his passion. The problems arose because of how he approached it.

Bob had never before shared his sailing dream with his wife, Linda. When offered the retirement package, he came home and told her he was retiring and they would be sailing around the world. When Linda seemed to hesitate, Bob said she could either come with him or he would be leaving without her. She relented, but you can see where this was heading.

Bob researched boats and decided on what he wanted to buy. He enrolled Linda and himself in sailing courses. Then, for the first time, he approached a financial advisor and described what he wanted to do, including withdrawing the high cost of the boat from his retirement funds, with all of the negative tax implications. Against advice, Bob forged ahead.

Linda and Bob were on the boat for only a couple of months when she decided it had been a bad idea from the beginning. She filed for divorce. The combination of the impulsive purchase of the boat and the cost of the divorce ruined what could have been a financially secure retirement life.

Margaret and James, who had only recently retired, had enjoyed playing golf together for some time. They played occasionally at local public courses. Through a friend, they were introduced to other golfing couples who played at the local country club. After playing at the club a few times, Margaret and James became enchanted with the feeling of being there, and they decided to join, despite the fact that initiation fees and dues stretched their planned retirement budget. They began socializing frequently with the country club crowd, further stretching their budget.

But their troubles were only beginning. They soon came to the conclusion that the only way to fit in was to buy a house located on the golf course near the country club, which they did. The cost of the house and furnishing it, as well as continuing to keep up with the lifestyles of other members, resulted in a complete depletion of their savings. The lure of instant gratification led to a lack of spending discipline and negatively affected the remainder of their retirement.

Barbara and Mike found themselves continuing to support their only son, Brad, who, in his mid-30s, had yet to "find himself." Brad had worked as an engineer and a realtor close to home, and then moved to California to become a hairstylist. Throughout this timeframe, he had been between jobs more than working, and Barbara and Mike had been supporting him in the range of $3000 to $4000 per month.

One day, Brad called from California saying he was planning to purchase a beauty parlor and asking if they would front him the money to do so. This financially secure retirement couple, who had found it difficult to say no to their son through the years, all the time watching their nest egg diminish faster than planned, were now forced to say no. Brad could not understand why his parents would not lend him the money.

Because Barbara and Mike had not had a conversation with their son to set expectations over the years, not only did they damage their retirement savings, they also damaged their relationship with Brad, who had no idea of the implications of his actions.

These three real-life scenarios are but a few examples of the effect of a lack of planning for and discipline to achieve financial security. You might argue that these people were pursuing their passions, enjoying connectedness, and nurturing their family. All of that would be true. The problem is that they did not create a holistic retirement plan that balanced both financial and non-financial elements. As you proceed through the remainder of the book and eventually build your plan, be sure to maintain the balance that will result in a holistic and achievable plan.

Happy and Comfortable

There are positive financial security examples as well. Susan and John developed a love for travel when their three children were young, exposing the children and themselves to adventuresome journeys while keeping expenses to a minimum by camping in the National Parks. The couple enjoyed the outdoors and found activities that met their needs and were of modest expenditure—biking, jogging, and tennis to complement their camping.

When the children were in college, but before John had retired, Susan wanted to expand her horizons by traveling outside the country. She also wanted to get more involved with volunteering. Susan suggested, and John agreed, that they would begin practicing retirement. They planned a series of two-week trips over the three years before John retired. They traveled to Europe, keeping expenses low by staying in Elder Hostels. They also began volunteering, taking vacation time closer to home to get involved with Habitat for Humanity. During the same timeframe, John joined a local cycling team, enjoying their long weekend bike rides.

Before John retired, he and Susan developed a budget for their upcoming years. They discussed the possibility of investing in a second home to spend part of the winters in Florida, but were concerned about the cost of doing so. Once John retired, they continued to travel from time-to-time, volunteer, and be active outdoors. When the real estate bubble burst, they began to research property in Florida. Because they knew what they could afford and because they had developed their shared retirement plan, John and Susan could take advantage of the situation. They purchased a nice condo at drastically discounted pricing.

They have a plan, are spending below their means, and doing everything they want to be doing. They are happy and comfortable.

Tom was an executive at a large corporation. He enjoyed his job, but he also looked forward to being able to the time when he could step away from the extensive hours at work and business trips away from home. Tom knew that his passion was to become a teacher, and he set his sights on teaching as a volunteer. Judy, Tom's wife, loved spending time with friends, but she wanted to spend more time with family, especially the grandchildren.

When Tom was approaching retirement, the couple met with a financial advisor and developed an integrated financial, estate, and tax plan that would support their goals. Doing so helped them understand what their resources really were. As a result, they also developed a non-financial plan.

They had vacationed in Hilton Head through the years and decided to buy a second home there. While walking on the beach one day, they spotted some property that they fell in love with. Shortly thereafter, they added the money they had for their second home to the money they got from the sale of their primary home and moved permanently to Hilton Head. Tom began teaching at a local university. The children and grandchildren visit often to take advantage of the beach environment, and the project of building the house on their new property brought Tom and Judy even closer together.

They had a plan, knew what their resources were, and took

advantage of the opportunity to achieve their retirement goals.

One could argue that couples with the means to be thinking about second homes should be financially secure. There are two things to point out, however. One is to contrast their stories with those in the previous section of this chapter. Those were people with above average financial means, who did not follow good financial security practices. The other is to recall the story of Helen and Walt Devaney from Chapter 4. They had modest means at best, yet achieved financial security by matching their lifestyle to their resources and continuing to do the things that were meaningful for them—friends, family, and travel.

Key Learning about "Financial Security"

1. While there is much more to retirement than "the money," having a written financial plan on how to fund your lifestyle is essential.
2. A financial planning expert can help you achieve financial security by coaching you on the many dimensions of finance and by holding you accountable to what you need to do (develop a budget, craft a will, save for the future, etc.).
3. Practicing solid financial management is critical, regardless of the amount of your nest egg. Live below your means, use credit wisely, and plan for contingencies.

Getting Started

1. Begin tracking your spending to establish a base from which to develop your retirement budget. Continue to track spending as long as necessary to get comfortable that you are living below your means.
2. Use your spending tracking as a base and understand which items may go up or down when you retire. Develop a base and "ideal" budget that reflects the costs of your retirement dreams.
3. Meet with several financial advisors and select one who can best work with you to develop your holistic financial plan, or find a friend or family member who can be a trusted expert.

4. Set a target date with your advisor or other expert by which the first draft of your financial plan will be complete.

5. Review your financial plans with others in your life who will be most affected by your choices.

"Financial Security" Planning Worksheet

Personal Assessment: Rate the following statement from 1 to 5:
1 = This statement in no way describes my level of financial security.
5 = This statement fully describes my level of financial security.

"I have a financial plan that will enable me to securely live the life I want (now and in the future)."

Rating: 1 2 3 4 5

Planning for "Financial Security"

What I will CONTINUE to do:

_____

_____

What I will START doing:

_____

_____

What I will STOP doing:

_____

_____

Other thoughts about Financial Security:

_____

_____

The one person in my life who can best help me to implement my immediate next step regarding Financial Security is

_____

Chapter 11

Connectedness

"When one tugs on a single string in nature,
he finds it attached to the rest of the world."
John Muir

"Only through our connectedness to others can
we really know and enhance the self. And only
though working on the self can we begin to
enhance our connectedness to others."
Harriet Goldhor Lerner

Do You Know?

Having a network of strong personal relationships is one of the most significant factors in determining your longevity, well-being, and happiness.

The average person today has 1.5 friends compared to three a decade ago.

Older adults who are more socially engaged are more likely to keep their intellectual skills and less likely to experience losses of motor skills like strength, speed, and dexterity.

About 40% of women in the U.S. over the age of 50 are single.

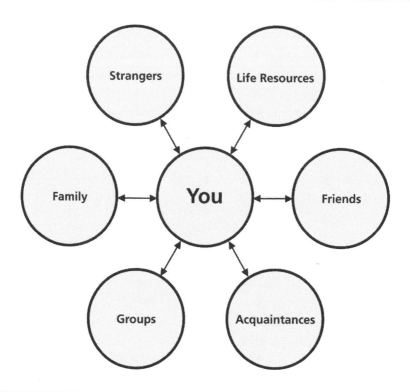

What is "Connectedness?"

Connectedness is initiating, building, and nurturing relationships. Connectedness is multidimensional, involving close personal relationships with family and friends, belonging to groups, linking to life resources, and relating to acquaintances and even strangers. To be fully and meaningfully connected, it is best to develop the full range of relationships, as pictured in this model.

Immediate family members are prime candidates for close mutually-supportive relationships, sharing unconditional love. Similar relationships can be cultivated among extended family. Family connectedness manifests itself in many ways; for example, supporting older relatives or being supported by younger ones, gaining nourishment from and giving nourishment to grandchildren, passing your legacy on to future generations, or just visiting with loved ones.

Friends, especially your "best friends," can be an additional source of meaningful relationships and support. Friends are those you can talk to about things that you may not be able to or want to share with others, including family. You may have or have had friends in the workplace, those who are more than colleagues and provide a willing ear when you need to vent. Studies have shown that a friend in the workplace can be the difference between leaving a job and finding it satisfying.

That being said, we have consistently heard from retirees that once they left the workplace, they have tended not to hear from former colleagues, even some they considered friends. They were surprised. They had expected these relationships to continue into retirement. If your workplace is or was your only source of friends, developing friends outside of work is a necessity.

Friends make a difference in your life. The Pew Research Center studied and reported the effect of friendships on the satisfaction level of retirees. The study found retirees who are very satisfied with their number of friends are nearly three times more likely to be happy than those who have fewer friends and are worried about their relationships.

Acquaintances are those you know well, but who fall short of being called a friend; yet they can be important sources of meaningful relationships in your life. Acquaintances can be high school classmates, neighbors, bridge group members, internet social networking partners, parents of your children's friends, workout partners at the gym, fellow churchgoers, or many other similar connections, including, as noted earlier, work colleagues. Acquaintances can also be a source of deeper friendships, a shift you will find important as you grow older and as life circumstance change. Current friends may move or pass away. There is even an argument for cultivating younger friends from your acquaintance list. Such friends will help keep you young and may be available to you longer than only those friends in your age group.

Groups are comprised of any number of people who share something in common, perhaps an activity or even a passion. Examples of groups are your church or synagogue, an organization for which you volunteer, a company for which you work, a sports team, or a club. Groups help you meet the need to belong, one of our basic human needs that, when satisfied, allows you to become all you can be.

Life resources are those who help you live on a daily basis, providing you with needed support. Examples are your doctor, postal worker, hairdresser, personal trainer, bank teller, neighborhood restaurant owner, and store clerk. The best example of the importance of this set of connections can be drawn from someone who moves to a new city and finds that all of the people who used to be available for support no longer are present to fill their functions. The connections were severed and new ones need to be formed. Life resources continue to be important in our latter years, perhaps even more so as we need additional assistance just for the activities of daily living.

The inclusion of strangers in our Connectedness model may surprise you. Think about the volunteer work you do or the charity you provide. You are likely anonymous to many, if not most, of the people to whom you are providing help. They are strangers, yet you have a relationship that nurtures you both.

It is important to note that "You" are in the center of this model. Part of connectedness is being in touch with yourself. An important benefit of planning for retirement is that as you go through the process, you cannot help but learn more about yourself, regardless of how self-aware you may be when you begin.

The intent of this chapter is to give you perspective that will guide your thinking with regards to your relationships across the full range of connection possibilities. With whom do you want to strengthen relationships? Who do you need to support you? Who do you want to befriend? Who are your life resources? To whom will you be giving back? Who do you want to make you smile?

We are Orphans

Leslie Berger did not feel good about his high school experience in the early 1960s. His exact words are, "I hated high school."

Yet, on December 17, 2002 at 12:31pm, Leslie Berger sent a message to every one of his University City (Missouri) High School classmates for whom he had an e-mail address. The simple, yet visionary message read, "Welcome to the UCity 1964 group. If you are in contact with any former classmates, please ask them to join the group. The more classmates who use the group the more fun everyone will have here."

It took about a year for Leslie's classmates to find the electronic discussion group and begin active messaging. Eventually, nearly 225 classmates would join. Between January and February 2004, the monthly message count jumped from 19 to 157 and continued to grow. In September 2004, the month before their 40-year reunion, there were 889 messages sent, almost 30 per day.

The message count from classmates all over the country and the world has passed 30,000 and grows daily. This is only an accounting of those messages posted to the group. Many postings prompt and even solicit private e-mail discussions outside the group, adding tens of thousands additional connections.

Leslie Berger on the Grand Canyon rim

Why did Leslie Berger send the message that began this communications phenomenon and launch himself into the center of connectedness of his classmates, despite the high school experience he hated? Several factors came together. Leslie had recently suffered a heart attack and his first stroke, which affected his eyesight and his gait; he could neither work nor drive. He had abruptly retired. Two months later, Leslie's mother passed away, his father having died in 1965.

Having been limited by the stroke and having lost his mom, he found that despite the support he received from Judy, Leslie's "love-of-his-life" wife, who was still working, and their grown children, he was "lonely." One classmate friend urged Leslie to "just put yourself out there" to get more connected. High school memories aside, Leslie counted on the common history and culture of his class and said to himself, "Why not?"

Leslie is now more than connected. He is a leader, and the class is more connected because of him. Leslie Berger belongs to something greater than himself; a class that cares about each other, supports classmates in need, and stays in touch on a daily basis.

Each of us belongs or has belonged to families, workgroups, synagogues, churches, volunteer organizations, bridge groups, golf foursomes, dinner clubs, baseball teams, support groups, book clubs, the audience that watches *American Idol*, college sororities, and on and on and on. Belonging feels good.

In his 1954 book, *Motivation and Productivity*, Abraham Maslow described the "hierarchy of human needs." As we satisfy our more basic human needs, like making sure we have enough to eat and that we are safe and secure, we can move up the hierarchy to satisfy higher-order needs. At the top of the hierarchy pyramid is self-actualization, becoming all that we can be.

In the middle of Maslow's pyramid is the human need to belong and be loved. Maslow wrote, "...there will emerge the love and affection and belongingness needs... Now the person will feel keenly, as never before, the absence of friends, or a sweetheart, or a wife, or children. He will hunger for affectionate relations with people in general, namely, for a group or family, and he will strive intensely to achieve this goal."

As our lives unfold, many of us have a need to belong that is increasingly intense and it manifests itself with a new level of engagement. What has happened over the years to increase our desire to search for belonging?

We have belonged to families in which our parents and grandparents and aunts and uncles provided us unconditional love. As we approach and enter retirement, our grandparents are gone; for many of us, one or both parents are gone. Others of us can see when that will happen all too soon. While the term is not generally used for mature adults, we are or about to become "orphans."

We reared our children, and for many of us, they are out of the house. They are building their own careers and families, having made many of us grandparents. Despite the joy of seeing our children doing well on their own, the reality is that they are no longer with us at home.

For the many years of our primary careers, those careers served to define us. When asked the question, "What do you do?" (a question that can be translated into "Who are you?"), our answer, while different for each of us in our different careers, sounded something like, "I work for Procter & Gamble."

We belong to and much of our identity is tied to the company, a business unit, a work team. Then retirement comes, and we no longer belong. Some of us are divorced or widowed. Many of us are single. Some of us have lost close friends to illness. Some have moved frequently, never having established long-term local relationships. Some of us are so busy just keeping up with life that we do not take the time to stay in touch with others.

As we age, therefore, we confront the reality that many of those connections in our lives that helped us meet our need to belong are no longer available. It will be important on *Your Retirement Quest* to find new connections to groups, organizations, and communities that will help you meet your need to belong, just as Leslie Berger did.

Super-Connector

Leslie's story tells of his now-strong connections with a group and with friends. The Connectedness model is also about nurturing supportive, mutually-beneficial, caring relationships with family, life resources, acquaintances, and even strangers.

As their parents have aged, both Keith and Sue Lawrence have seen the critical importance of having a strong support network of people nearby. Sue's and Keith's parents live 100 miles and 600 miles away, respectively. Keith's father, Howard, was ill for a few years before he passed away in 2002. Keith's mother, Pat, cared for her husband at home, but this became exhausting, and she needed support. Fortunately, over the years, Pat had developed a large circle of caring friends and neighbors, who mobilized to provide the needed support—both the physical support for Howard and the emotional support for Pat.

Recently, Sue's mother, Jane, required urgent medical attention. Up to that point, Sue's father, Jack, had shouldered the responsibility, but Jane's condition required more skilled nursing care. It was not initially obvious where to find the needed care, and the first attempts proved to be exhausting as well as frustrating for everyone involved. Through persistent effort, Sue and her dad were able to identify the right contacts, who helped find the professional resources Jane needed.

Howard's and Jane's illnesses taught Keith and Sue and, hopefully, all of us that connections with life resources are critical, not only to the person who is ill, but also to his or her family. They also learned that it is best, to the extent possible, to ensure these connections are in place in anticipation of the need. Keith's and Sue's experiences with their parents also reinforced the value of lifelong friends and the closeness of family.

Nancy Riesz is a founding partner of LifeScape, LLC and has been an executive consultant for more than 20 years; certified by the International Coach Federation. Nancy is also what is known as a "super-connector." You may not know Nancy, but you probably know someone like her; someone who seems to know everyone and who everyone seemingly knows. We asked Nancy how she thought about connectedness. This is what she said:

"I cannot imagine being happy without other people, lots of them, in my life. Not only have relationships in my life nurtured my heart and soul, they have opened doors, introduced me to new adventures and ways of thinking, expanded my knowledge and awareness, provided insights, and produced many hours of fun. My friends have always been available sources of support, energy, encouragement, and play. I cannot imagine getting through the seven and one-half weeks my mom was in ICU without the prayers and inspiration of my friends."

Nancy Riesz with Kristin, her best friend

Many are natural connectors, while others may need to take conscious, proactive steps to make and sustain relationships that are and will be so important to living fully in retirement. Nancy is a natural, and her network of connections is growing all the time.

Nancy continued, "Developing connections with others is not something I consciously think about. It is as natural for me to introduce myself and get to know people as it is for me to walk and talk. I often find one connection leads to many others. Several years ago, I shared with my friend, Linda, that I was learning to play golf as a way to spend more time with my dad, but I also wanted to find other women with whom I could enjoy the game. Linda suggested I join EWGA (Executive Women Golf Association), which I did. I played regularly with 14 women that summer and learned another reason I love golf; it's a great social activity.

"That recommendation by Linda to join EWGA led to me meeting and building relationships with many more women. Here's how that worked. After playing with the first group of EWGA, I volunteered to start a new league at a course closer to home. Through this new league, I met Mela, who invited me to speak at an executive women's lunch program she was planning. Through this presentation, I have a new close friend, Susan; have developed multiple business opportunities; and found new adventures, like being introduced to 'glow golf,' playing golf in the dark—all from that first question I asked my friend, Linda."

Nancy values connections, seeks them out, nurtures them, and sustains them. Her life is enriched by the multitude of relationships she has developed. The intent of sharing her story, however, is not to suggest that each of us needs to be a super-connector. Rather, it is to show that when you are open to connections, they are available to you and can make a meaningful difference in your life, perhaps taking it in a new and different direction.

Ann Spector, Alan's wife, has always been interested in her ancestry and places family high on her values list. Even before she retired, Ann began to research her father's family tree. As she did so, she found relatives all over the world who were interested in finding and sharing information, joining Ann in the effort to identify every family member they could. It soon became evident that merely capturing the data was not sufficient. Connections around the world were becoming stronger. A family reunion was in order. In March 2007, branches of her father's family converged on New York—coming from Israel, England, South Africa, and all around the United States. Throughout the family tree project, which Ann keeps active, new and strong connections have been fostered among cousins who never previously met and, in some cases, did not even know the others existed, sometimes in the same community. Ann and many members of her family, some she has yet to meet, are living more fulfilling lives for having connected.

In early 2007, Alan Spector and Keith Lawrence became deeply involved at the inception of the Cincinnati Initiative to Reduce Violence (CIRV), a community effort to reverse the upward trend in homicides involving violent street groups. During this effort, we became acquainted with city government officials, police officers, social service agency personnel, criminal justice academics, and members of the community at large. One of the groups we met was on the front line of the effort, out on the streets working directly with the target population. These "Street Workers" were themselves ex-offenders, who had been involved in street violence and had served prison terms, but who had turned their lives around and were now working to help others. Both of us are better off for having been acquainted with the "Street Workers," who reinforced for us that major change is possible in a person's life.

By extension, we were also connected to members of the violent street groups. While we met some of these young men over the course of the initiative, they were, in general, strangers to us. Yet, what we were doing was positively affecting their lives, and therefore, ours.

The story with the initiative does not end there. The network of connections expanded. Keith and others realized that working to curb violence required making an intervention much earlier in a person's life; before he chose to become involved in a local street gang.

While doing research to find a good approach, the planners learned about and connected with "The Lifeplan Institute," a group that had already validated a methodology and embarked on an effort to touch the lives of ten million middle school students, helping them make better life choices. As a result of this new connection, Keith helped bring "Lifeplan" to Cincinnati. Twelve local people have been trained in the technique, and the effort is underway with resounding results.

These stories provide but a few examples of connections with family, friends, groups, life resources, acquaintances, and strangers. Each connection has enhanced lives and promises to continue to do so.

The False (?) Promise of Technology

The jury is still out on the value technology brings to the connectedness of our lives. Many people have stories about finding a long-lost relative on Facebook or being readily able to communicate with relatives in far-off places via e-mail or Skype. Leslie Berger connected high school classmates scattered around the country and the world. It is hard to argue that video-calling a grandson that you see only a few times a year or electronically comparing family tree notes with a newly-found relative in Cape Town, South Africa is a bad thing.

However, many of us have hundreds of "friends" on Facebook, are connected with hundreds via LinkedIn, receive hundreds of e-mails each day, follow hundreds on Twitter, belong to multiple electronic discussion groups, and text incessantly. All of these have their place and may serve to build our networks of acquaintances and even strangers. That being said, common sense tells us that while we may be connected technologically, we may not really be connected in the most meaningful ways. The connections that make the most difference in our lives are those that are deep, rich relationships; people who miss you when you do not show up; those who really care when they ask how you are doing; friends who "have your back;"

people who you want to see face-to-face.

Utilize the technology for what it does best, but do not be seduced by it to the exclusion of creating the deep relationships that will have the most meaning in your life. Make your contacts with these relationships as personal as possible. Sometimes you have to "disconnect to connect."

We do not want to come across as stodgy, old-school, regressive, or just plain out of touch. We know that an increasing percentage of couples are meeting electronically first, then establishing more lasting personal relationships. We know that close friends and family who live in different geographies find it easier and less expensive to stay in touch between visits and phone calls. We worked for a global company and had bosses, subordinates, and colleagues on the other side of the world with whom we collaborated to run the business. We know technology enables us to run our LifeScape Solutions™ business and manage the co-authorship of this book from 350 miles apart.

We also know that personal contact cannot be replaced when it comes to family, good friends, and colleagues. It is the reason classes have reunions even though they can now keep in touch via e-mail and up to date through their web sites. It is the reason grandparents visit grandchildren across the country even though they can see each other through a video call. It is the reason long-distance work colleagues travel to meet face-to-face periodically despite being able to meet over the phone. It is the reason that we met frequently through the process of writing this book despite being able to share ideas, drafts, and edits electronically.

That being said, George Ford, Chief Economist of the Phoenix Center, in testimony before Congress, said that the Center found that accessing the internet reduces the frequency of depression among seniors by up to 20%. Why? As we age, there is a tendency for us to become more withdrawn from society. While not the only or, perhaps, the best resolution to increasing isolation among seniors, the internet can become a source of connectedness. This does not argue for everyone achieving their connectedness via on-line relationships; rather, it argues that any increase in a person's connectedness can be beneficial.

Key Learning about "Connectedness"

1. Having meaningful relationships is an important element of retirement happiness, as well as of a longer, higher quality life.
2. Being connected means having a full network of family, friends, acquaintances, groups, life resources, and even strangers.
3. Being more socially engaged with others helps you retain your mental faculties as you age.

Getting Started

1. Seek to strengthen the relationships with those who are already close to you in your life. Be clear about who they are and reach out to invest yourself in being there for them. Take the initiative; do not wait. Give them a call, listen patiently to an issue in their lives, or get together to just hang out. Let go of any resentments that drain your vitality.
2. Look for opportunities to serve others in need by offering your skills and experience. It could be as simple as staffing a local soup kitchen on Saturday mornings. If you love to plan, get involved in organizing reunions and other events for your high school class or college fraternity. The opportunities are endless and can fit your particular interests and needs.
3. Use the Connectedness model to look at your current network and see what might be missing. Do you have the life resources you need, like a financial planner? Are there groups you would enjoy? Is your network of friends and acquaintances extensive and diverse? Do you know your neighbors? If not, think about forming a dinner club or hosting a street party. Are you sufficiently connected with your family? Is there someone working on your family tree and, if not, should you recruit another family member to work on it with you?
4. Look for ways to be an even better friend than you are.
5. Look for opportunities to befriend people younger than you.
6. Make a commitment to yourself to "reach out" to strangers—smiling opening a door, saying thank you. It will not only brighten their day, but yours as well.

"Connectedness" Planning Worksheet

Personal Assessment: Rate the following statement from 1 to 5:
1 = This statement is far from describing how I am connected.
5 = This statement fully describes how I am connected.

"I am missed by others if I don't show up. I have others who I can lean on."

Rating: 1 2 3 4 5

Planning for "Connectedness"
What I will CONTINUE to do:

_____

_____

What I will START doing:

_____

_____

What I will STOP doing:

_____

_____

Other thoughts about Connectedness:

_____

_____

The one person in my life who can best help me to implement my immediate next step regarding Connectedness is

_____

Chapter 12

Giving Back

"If you have much, give of your wealth.
If you have little, give of your heart."
Arab Proverb

"If you wish to experience peace,
provide peace for another."
Tenzin Gyatso

Do You Know?

Only 27% of retirees do community service.

Less than 4% of retirees invest more than four hours per week helping others.

On average, retirees spend 43 hours per week watching TV.

The happiest people on the planet are more "other centered."

What is "Giving Back?"

Giving back is believing that you are part of something greater than yourself, then acting on that belief.

Our culture frequently signals that we should be thinking only about ourselves. Madonna sang, "...we are living in a material world." Gordon Gekko proclaimed, "...greed, for lack of a better word, is good. Greed is right, greed works..."

The good news is that countless people give of themselves for others in countless ways, from sharing a simple smile to giving significant time, energy, and resources to those in need. The better news is that the benefits of giving accrue to the giver as well as the receiver.

Carolyn Schwartz, a research professor from the University of Massachusetts Medical School, was investigating the effects of multiple sclerosis sufferers receiving monthly peer-support phone calls from fellow sufferers. While those receiving the support showed some small benefit, Schwartz found the real beneficiaries were those lending a supportive ear. They experienced significant improvements in the quality of their lives, more so than those they were helping.

Schwartz (and others) built on this learning by conducting research with over 2000 representative people across the country, and, in 2003, published "Altruistic Social Interest Behaviors Are

Associated With Better Mental Health." The conclusion of the study was, "Helping others is associated with higher levels of mental health, above and beyond the benefits of receiving help..."

Another indicator of the power of giving back was the world response to the devastating 2010 earthquake in Haiti. Hundreds of millions of dollars and other humanitarian assistance poured in from around the world despite the tragedy occurring during the world's greatest economic downturn since the Great Depression. People are yearning to help and give back to the world.

The English author, A. A. Milne, creator of *Winnie the Pooh*, wrote, "In the quiet hours when we are alone and there is nobody to tell us what fine fellows we are, we come sometimes upon a moment in which we wonder, not how much money we are earning, nor how famous we have become, but what good we are doing."

Giving back is doing good for others.

Million Points of Light

Every year, Lili and Jerry Sachar, host a Friday-after-Thanksgiving dinner for their extended family. Depending on who is in town from around the county, there are between 40 and 70 at the party. Lasagna, salad, rolls, and desserts feed the gatherers, who are still stuffed from Thanksgiving dinners the evening before. Food, laughter, and family story-telling abound.

Lili Sachar

For years, Lili has volunteered a couple of times each week at a local Food Pantry that supports the needy in the community. During the recent difficult economic times, the Food Pantry was stressed and could not meet the geometrically growing needs. Shelves were empty, and sadly, some left the food pantry with less than what they really needed for their families.

Lili put the word out—the "price of admission" to the annual post-Thanksgiving feast would be a bag of groceries for the Food Pantry. As her extended family came through the door, each gladly put his or her contribution in the boxes waiting to be filled. The next morning, Lili took the large accumulation of food to the Pantry to be distributed to those in need.

Not only did Lili create the opportunity for her family to give once, but her compassion and personal commitment to give back to her community was taught to young and old. She is a role model for giving back.

Ron Unell retired from his career as a CPA and founding partner of his firm. While thrilled to be retired and enjoying his new-found freedom, Ron was also searching for ways to best use his time, resources, and skills. He cares deeply about children, and when a cousin exposed him to a non-profit organization, "Caring for Kids," Ron was hooked. Caring for Kids "provides essential resources to meet the urgent needs of children involved in the Family Court system...(and) seeks to enhance the lives of children who have either been abused, neglected or considered 'at risk.'" Ron is now on the Board of Directors of the organization. He is using his CPA skills to help them with their financial challenges and is ready to do any hands-on activity where he can contribute.

Ron and Elaine Unell

Ron's wife, Elaine, is a retired teacher, having taught kindergarten, first grade, and a gifted student program over her 33-year career. To continue to utilize her skills and to give back in retirement, Elaine now volunteers with the Gifted Resource Council (GRC), a not-for-profit education agency whose purpose it is to bring together the resources of the community, schools, and parents to help bright and talented children achieve their potential. Elaine volunteers from September through March to help the GRC plan and run its annual Academic Challenge Cup Competitions. Her volunteer work ranges from event planning to setup/cleanup, to judging, to creating posters, to whatever it takes to have successful competitions. Elaine both gives and gets from her efforts to help the 1700 to 2000 participants each year. As she says, "...it keeps my mind stimulated and helps me to feel I am helping others."

Pat Lawrence is 82 years old, looks to be in her 60s, and acts like she is 35. She has had a rich life, much of it guided by her passion of giving of herself to others: her Lord, her husband of 53 years (who has passed away), her three sons and daughters-in-law, her six grandchildren, other family members, and her countless friends. She takes great pride in playing music every week at a local nursing home. Pat is an exceptional pianist, and the nursing home residents look forward to hearing her play. When she is away, they miss her and the joy she brings to their world. Through giving back, she uses her gift of music, touches the lives of others, feels valued, and has a lot of fun in the process.

Pat Lawrence

Lili, Ron, Elaine, and Pat are but a few of the literally millions of examples of those who have found ways to contribute to their communities by giving of their time, talent, and resources. You likely personally know others who are also great examples. They are not Bill Gates or Warren Buffet, who generously contribute billions of dollars to worthy causes. Rather, they are among the "millions of points of light," to paraphrase President George H. W. Bush. In his 1989 inaugural address, President Bush said, "I have spoken of a thousand points of light...spread like stars throughout the Nation, doing good. We will work hand-in-hand...in taking part and pitching in."

More Blessed to Give

If you do not want to take the Bible literally when it reads, "It is more blessed to give than to receive (Acts 20:35)," consider the research to support the point. In 2008, researchers from the University of British Columbia and the Harvard Business School reported "Spending Money on Others Promotes Happiness." The study was conducted among over 600 Americans, who were asked to rate their general happiness. Through several different experiments, the researchers assessed the effects of income level and "prosocial" spending on happiness. Prosocial spending is that which you spend on others (e.g., charitable donations). The study had three revealing conclusions:

1. People tend to adapt to the stable circumstances of their lives, thereby not extracting happiness from higher income levels versus lower ones.
2. Even though prosocial spending was less than ten percent of personal spending, it was a significant factor in predicting happiness. By inference, contributing time and skill to give back to the community through prosocial action will also bring happiness.
3. These results and conclusions were shared with a different sampling of people. Despite knowing what the study found, this new group still believed their happiness would be primarily driven by their own income levels and what they spent on themselves. One could conclude that in order to move toward a happier, more fulfilling life, we must make a conscious effort to give back through prosocial spending of resources, time, and skills. This does not necessarily come naturally.

In a separate and smaller study in Eugene, Oregon, research subjects were given $100 and told either they would be making a mandatory transfer of funds to a local food bank or they could voluntarily give to the same charity. Using Magnetic Resonance Imaging to measure the participants, researchers detected activity changes in an area of the brain that has been previously associated with the brain's response to rewarding stimuli, such as viewing pictures of loved ones. The reward reaction was most intense with the voluntary giving.

A survey of 30,000 American households by the Social Capital Community Benchmark Survey found people who gave money to charity were 43% more likely to be "very happy" about their lives than non-givers. The survey also found that volunteers were 42% more likely to be very happy than non-volunteers. It did not matter whether donations of time or money went to secular or religious causes; givers were far happier than non-givers.

Research aside, it is likely intuitive that helping others will make you feel good, while also contributing to the greater good. Giving back to family, friends, and community that have given so much to you is a meaningful, fulfilling, self-improving activity. "It is more blessed to give than to receive."

Endless Opportunities

Retirees and those nearing and planning for retirement have the experience, wisdom, skills, time, and resources to make the world a better place. No one is better positioned to give back to families, friends, and communities than retirees.

In 2007, Keith's wife, Sue, retired after 33 rewarding years teaching elementary school, allowing her to dedicate a significant amount of time giving back to others. In addition to caring for her family and friends on a daily basis, Sue has been blessed with a host of opportunities to apply her time and talents for others. Sue leads several women's Bible study groups and volunteers at her church's Healing Center. When she learned of a group home that was formed to help young, at-risk women in need, Sue immersed herself in the program; providing mentoring, supervision, and friendship, making a difference in the lives of the young women and, thereby, making the world a better place. As time allows, Sue also volunteers at a local Hospice.

In her 80s, Leah Friedman wrote her memoirs and had the book printed and bound to give her children and grandchildren a perspective of their history and to share her legacy with them.

Harold Sanger volunteers with his local city government, believing it is best to work in the system rather than complain about it from the outside.

Paula Sigel loves to collect antique silver and other objects of art. She uses her knowledge to give back to her community by volunteering at her local art museum.

The *New York Times* has reported that more than 25 million people age 55 and older volunteer in some capacity. The *Times* further reported that while the community benefits, so do retirees who have an increased sense of purpose, sustained contact with their community, and an increased level of self-esteem and energy. This good news is tempered by the realization that if 25 million are volunteering, about 50 million are not.

Federal Judge Ron Gould volunteers with the Chief Seattle Council of the Boy Scouts of America. Ron became an Eagle Scout while in high school and has now received the Distinguished Eagle Scout Award from the National Boy Scouts of America for his volunteer efforts.

Irene Mescheloff welcomes new immigrants from North America at the airport when they arrive to settle in Israel, remembering the value of the support she received when she immigrated.

Ronna Levy is a Board member and cheerleader for Angie's Spa, a non-profit organization founded in memory of Ronna's daughter, who died of breast cancer. Angie's Spa provides free spa services to cancer patients undergoing chemotherapy.

Retired business executives around the world are donating their strategic planning, leadership, and management systems skills to non-profit organizations.

Churches, synagogues, mosques, and other religious institutions are supported by legions of volunteers, who offer their time and resources to make a difference in the lives of fellow congregants and their communities.

Schools, hospitals, libraries, social service organizations, and community initiatives rely heavily on volunteers to staff positions requiring a broad range of skills and time availability.

Children dedicate their time and resources to care for aging parents. Grandparents pitch in to take care of grandchildren. Relatives help family members dealing with illness. Friends bring meals to an ailing neighbor or drive a recovering friend to therapy.

The opportunities to give back are endless. They can take as little or as much time as you have. They can require manual labor or high-level technical skills. Opportunities can include financial considerations, but many, if not most, cost nothing but your compassion, time, experience, energy, and skill.

Doing Good Together

What if we told you that there is a giving back opportunity that is also linked with another meaningful aspect of retirement? Certainly not all of us are grandparents, but many of us are or will be. Surveys have shown that for those who are grandparents, the number one activity that brings meaning to their lives is spending time with their grandchildren.

In 2004, after her book, *A Busy Family's Guide to Volunteering: Do Good, have fun, make a difference as a family*, was published, Jenny Friedman founded a non-profit organization to bring her vision and passion to life. Jenny is now the Executive Director of "Doing Good Together" (www.DoingGoodTogether.org), whose mission is to, "inspire, encourage, and equip families to volunteer together...[and to] raise children who are compassionate, aware of social issues, and are instilled with a lifelong habit of giving."

To date, the focus of "Doing Good Together" has been the nuclear family, working closely with parents and children. Jenny and her organization are beginning to see the future of facilitating the powerful grandparent/grandchild partnership to help bring their mission to life. Many retirees have the time, resources, and, certainly, the motivation to spend time with their grandchildren to give back to their communities while passing on a legacy of giving at the same time.

Wayne Urbaniak is a retired special education teacher, who, since retiring in 2004, has been delivering Meals on Wheels in South Minneapolis on the same route every Tuesday. Retirement has also given Wayne and his wife, Kathy, more time to spend with their six grandchildren, five who live in the Minneapolis/St. Paul area. Wayne has creatively combined his Meals on Wheels volunteer effort with the love he has for his family by involving his grandchildren.

When each grandchild is old enough to buckle and unbuckle his or her own seat belt, he or she is eligible to help Wayne deliver the meals. Those who have helped him range in age from four to eight. The three-year old, Delaney, has already begun to lobby for wanting to help and will soon.

Wayne Urbaniak with three of his six Meals on Wheels grandchildren, Landon (8) and Brooks (5), who have delivered with Grandpa, and Delaney (3), who cannot wait for her turn.

The grandchildren take turns joining Grandpa on the route. Even the grandson who lives in Tucson, Arizona looks forward to helping when he is in town. The children love the routine for many reasons. They are proud to be serving those in need, and eight-year-old Landon even presented how the program works to a church group to help influence others to participate. They enjoy the responsibility of helping match the meal recipient's name and address to make sure the right hot meal goes to the right person. And, importantly, they love doing all of this with Grandpa, who takes each Tuesday's helper to lunch after completing the route.

Wayne Urbaniak's grandchildren bring meaning to his life and he to theirs. When he and the children join together to give back to those in need, it is, as Wayne says, "a blessing for the people we deliver to and a blessing for our family."

Key Learning about "Giving Back"

1. Giving back to family, friends, and community will not only help the recipients, but will improve your life as well.
2. There are countless ways for you to give back, allowing you to find ways that are consistent with your talents and your passions and helping you personally grow and have fun.

Getting Started

1. Search for and begin a giving back opportunity that is meaningful but will take a minimal amount of time. If you have not been volunteering, start small. This will get you started toward bigger opportunities.
2. Let your friends and family know that you are looking for opportunities to serve others, while also actively listening for opportunities from other sources.
3. As you get started, partner with a friend or family member who has similar interests. For example, join a church community service activity together. While at the church, ask what other opportunities there are.

"Giving Back" Planning Worksheet

Personal Assessment: Rate the following statement from 1 to 5:
1 = This statement is far from describing how I am giving back.
5 = This statement fully describes how I am giving back.

"I am engaged in activities that make a meaningful difference to others."

Rating: 1 2 3 4 5

Planning for "Giving Back"

What I will CONTINUE to do:

_____

_____

What I will START doing:

_____

_____

What I will STOP doing:

_____

_____

Other thoughts about Giving Back:

_____

_____

The one person in my life who can best help me to implement my immediate next step regarding Giving Back is

_____

Chapter 13

Passions

*"Nothing great in the world has ever been
accomplished without passion."*
Fredrich Hebbel

*"Doing what you love is the cornerstone of
having abundance in your life."*
Dr. Wayne Dyer

Do You Know?

One of the top three regrets of people nearing death is summarized by one who said, "I wish I had taken more risk to pursue my dreams. I let my fears stop me."

The first half of life can be learning what you love to do—the second half can be really enjoying those things.

Employee happiness in the workplace is less than 50% and has been falling for several years. Their jobs have lost meaning; people are unable to pursue their passions at work.

Your passions can be developed in your youth or later in life; the key is to identify and pursue them.

What are "Passions?"

When we chose the word "Passions," we were concerned that we would overstate our intent. Passion is a strong word, described as "intense emotion" or "intense enthusiasm." None of us can be, by that definition, passionate about everything we do. Much of what we do, by necessity and choice, is rote daily living. Some things we choose to do just because they are fun or for other reasons.

Most of us, however, do have interests we are passionate about. How might you know when you have discovered our true passions? Here are some simple tests.

- Is the interest closely associated with your life's purpose?
- Do you lose track of time when you are engaged in the pursuit?
- Are you deeply inquisitive about it; constantly seeking to learn more?
- Do you appreciate others who are pursuing the activity?
- Do you want to jump out of bed in the morning to get started?

Some retirees rediscover the things they were passionate about when they were young. Many are inspired by asking themselves, "What was I passionate about when I was ten years old?" Recall the baseball and books passions from Alan Spector's story. Others discover their passions later in life. Some passions grow slowly; others rush up on you and take your breath away.

When retired, you have the opportunity and time to identify your passions and pursue them. In the 2007 movie, *The Bucket List*, main characters Edward Cole and Carter Chambers, both terminally ill, are sharing a hospital room. They decide to leave the hospital to do all the things they have wanted to do before they die; their bucket list. Instead of saying, "if only," would it not be great to say:

"I flew in a glider for the first time."

"I planted the garden I've always wanted."

"After all these years doing crossword puzzles, I've constructed one for my grandchildren."

"I am involved in local theater productions."

"I have taken my grandson to see a game in every major league park on the East Coast."

"The quilting classes I'm taking are really paying off."

"I finally have the woodworking shop set up in the basement."

"I've loved books all of my life, and I finally completed my first manuscript."

"I can't wait to get back to the pottery wheel."

What were you passionate about when you were ten years old? What makes you get up and get going in the morning? What have you discovered as an intense interest in later years? What activity makes time stop for you? What is on your bucket list? These are your passions. Identify and pursue them—now.

Tony Robbins, among the most influential motivational speakers and self-help authors, ends each of his sessions with, "Live life with passion."

HO HO HO!

Ron Podolsky was a big, strong high school football player with a marvelous and persistent sense of humor. He was the kind of guy everyone wanted to be around, because he just made you feel good in his presence. Ron was on the way to building his career, life, and family, when, in 1975, the first of a string of setbacks presented itself.

Just six weeks after his wedding, at age 28, Ron was diagnosed with a brain tumor in the frontal lobe. The operation to remove the tumor seemed to be successful; however, a decade later, the tumor returned. The second brain operation successfully prevented the return of the tumor, but left Ron blind in one eye.

In 1984, a fire truck was speeding down the highway. While this is not an unusual occurrence, in this case, it was on the wrong side of the road. It collided head-on with Ron's car, breaking almost every bone in his body. It took Ron nearly five years to recover from his injuries and from the multitude of surgeries required to put him back together.

Ron went on to work as a loan counselor for 15 years before the residual effects of his injuries caught up with him, making it impossible for him to continue. In 2004, at age 57, Ron retired and began a search for what he could do to make his life meaningful.

The positive attitude that had sustained him through his brain tumor and the car accident was still an integral part of his makeup. Despite being unable to walk or stand for long periods of time, he was determined to find his place.

With the help of the Center for Head Injury Services, Ron indeed found that place. He had been entertaining those around him his whole life and has a talent and passion for making people laugh. He also has a passion for music and a talent for playing the piano. Ron built on his passions and began playing and entertaining at special events.

Ron Podolsky

During the Christmas season of 2008, for example, Ron walked into a local nursing home and asked if they would like him to play the piano for their holiday party. When the nursing home manager asked Ron if he would also be willing to play Santa Claus, he enthusiastically replied, "HO, HO, HO!"

Ron later said, "It was exhilarating! I got a chance to entertain 100 people by playing the piano."

Ron now books frequent performances at that nursing home and others in the area. He could have given up at many times in his life. Yet Ron's attitude, good humor, and, importantly, the pursuit of his passions merged to add meaning to his retirement life.

Doing What the Heart Desires

Harry Bunn had a 35-year career of Federal government service, including three years in the military, one of which was served in Vietnam. He built his career using his accounting degree, starting with the government as an IRS internal auditor. He then moved on to auditing stints with the US Army at Fort Riley and with the US Finance and Accounting Center. When Harry retired in 2007, he lived in Indianapolis with his wife, Marsha, and had been the Chief of Payroll and then the Chief of Travel for US Customs and Border Protection.

Harry was good at what he did and, one might assume he would continue to pursue very left-brain activities in retirement. That is exactly what Harry did *not* do.

When he was in college, Harry was exposed to and became very interested in numerology, astrology, and the I Ching, an ancient and classic Chinese divination text. He continued to learn more over the years. Then, in the mid-1990s, passion came together with inspiration.

Harry was having a conversation with a clairvoyant friend, and, seemingly out of nowhere, declared that he was interested in becoming a medium/psychic and spiritual advisor. With that self-awareness, Harry began studying more intently and planning for retirement, at which time he knew he would follow his dreams.

Since retiring in 2007, Harry has made a number of significant changes in his life. He and Marsha have moved to Sedona, Arizona, the location which many believe has the greatest concentration of spiritual vortexes. In Sedona, he has started a business as a medium/clairvoyant in which he does readings, numerology charts, and flame messages, a form of clairvoyant readings. He also offers vortex tours.

Consistent with the other changes in his life, he also changed his name to Hari.

Hari Bunn

Whether or not you subscribe to Hari's beliefs, it is powerful to subscribe to his insightful advice about retirement. "To get ready for retirement is to take a serious look inside of yourself and identify what makes you happy/content with life and what you do...it is about finding out what you were really meant to do...retirement is where one goes to expand one's being/soul through doing what the heart desires."

While Hari did not use the word "passion," he, in essence, defined passion in retirement.

Personal Renaissance

Ron Podolsky had been passionate about entertaining people and playing music since he was a child. Hari Bunn became interested in clairvoyance in college and developed his passion further over time. Some say that retirement fulfillment comes from pursuing the passions you had when you were ten or thereabouts. Others discover their passions later in life. Regardless of what your passions are or when they originated, a key to a fulfilling retirement is to pursue them.

Logan Franklin is a retired publisher who maintains a web site (www.senior-exercise-central.com) and blog about fitness for seniors. Logan began exercising in his teens and has never stopped. At age 71, he is both pursuing his personal passion and giving back by sharing it with others.

Logan, who has written two books, *Gray Iron: A Training Guide for Senior Men and Women* and *Living the Fitness Lifestyle*, wrote an article for his web site entitled, "Retirement Bliss." In the article, he captures the essence of identifying your passions, then pursuing them. His concluding paragraph reads, "Probably your interests are very different than mine. But somewhere in each of us the interests are there, only waiting to be rediscovered and released. One good way to uncover them is by looking backward to your childhood and adolescence. Recall the thoughts, activities, and dreams that sent your imagination and spirit soaring. Those are your clues. Develop interests related to them and you are likely to experience a personal renaissance."

Logan says we will know we have identified our passions when our "…imagination and spirit [are] soaring." Rock and Roll Hall-of-Famer, Herb Alpert, is still touring in his mid-70s. While he has retired some of his songs (e.g., "Lonely Bull" and "Spanish Flea") and no longer is backed by the Tijuana Brass, Alpert goes on. He is fortunate to have found his passion early in life and then to make it his life's work.

When asked why he continues to play, Alpert's answer gives us another way to assess whether we have found our passions. He answers, "It's odd, but playing the trumpet gives me energy."

What gives you energy? What makes you want to get up and start your day with vigor each morning? Those are the things about which you are passionate. Pursue them and "experience a personal renaissance."

Healing Touch

Carol Strelic, who is 60, lives in Brick, New Jersey, where she has had a satisfying career as a massage therapist and exercise class leader. Over the years, she has also developed a passion for and has been studying holistic health, including techniques like healing touch. Her passion and life experiences have combined to guide her to a new life pursuit. Carol's own words best describe her transformation.

"They say with age comes wisdom. I'm not sure if my new direction falls into that category, but it is, most certainly, a gift that can only come with age. It is the gift of perspective, the ability to look back upon your life and see, with clarity, the milestones, the choices, the moments that have led to your now. I see it like this: you're watching the movie of your life on the white screen of your mind, and the reel slows down at the significant events; Encountering a certain someone, a piece of conversation, a book that finds its way into your hands, a choice to go or stay, to follow or rebel. Minor moments or momentous occasions, with the gift of age and perspective, these appear now with clarity as turning points that have brought you to the life you are living today. My movie could be titled, *Tender Nudges from the Hand of God.*

Carol Strelic

"The life I am living today includes giving compassionate touch to people in hospice. I am, by training and eleven years of hands-on experience, a certified massage therapist. Although not officially in the ranks of the retired (60 years old and still in need of a regular paycheck), this might be what a successful retirement might feel like. It certainly doesn't feel like 'work.' I love what I do. Each day, I know my heart will open to and my hands will touch those who need both. I am in service to others and am, sometimes, moved to tears by the gratitude I feel.

"Although countless moments of my life led me to my passion, three 'momentous occasions' hold obvious and great significance—the early and appalling death of my mom, the at-home-with-hospice death of my dad, and the natural, even beautiful death of my dear, dear aunt. Great losses, great sadness, surely. But, I think, their direct connection to what I do is the fact that I was not present for them as they died. I was not there to stroke their hand, to whisper in their ear, 'It's okay. You can go. You will be with me, in me always.'

"So, I give to them as I touch others. I carry them with me into the homes I enter. I remain connected to them in love and that connects me to those I touch with love. The truth is I am the one who is touched."

Key Learning about "Passions"

1. Identifying and pursuing your passions lead to peak life experiences.
2. Your passions may be those things you loved to do when you were young or they may be newly-found. In either case, incorporating them in your life plan is an integral part of a fulfilling retirement.
3. Following your passions will, in most cases, bring other benefits to your life—connecting you with others, having fun, improving your ability to take risks and manage change.
4. Retirement can be the best time in your life to pursue your passions, because you have time, energy, and resources you may not have had while working and building your family.

Getting Started

1. Ask yourself the question, "What was I passionate about when I was ten years old?" The answer may lead you to rediscover your true passions in retirement and help you begin to define your "bucket list."
2. Think about the five passion test questions from earlier in this chapter. These will guide you to identifying your true passions so that you can pursue them further and more deeply.
3. When you identify one of your untapped passions, decide what you can do tomorrow to move you one step forward and add that step to your personal plan.
4. Be willing to let go of things that no longer provide excitement in your life. These are the things that go in your "Stop" plan.

"Passions" Planning Worksheet

Personal Assessment: Rate the following statement from 1 to 5:
1 = This statement in no way describes how my passions affect me.
5 = This statement fully describes how my passions affect me.

"I jump out of bed in the morning excited about my day."

Rating: 1   2   3   4   5

Planning for "Passions"
What I will CONTINUE to do:

_____

_____

What I will START doing:

_____

_____

What I will STOP doing:

_____

_____

Other thoughts about Passions:

_____

_____

The one person in my life who can best help me to implement my immediate next step regarding Passions is

_____

Chapter 14

Growth

"Man's mind, once stretched by a new idea, never regains its original dimensions."
Oliver Wendell Holmes, Jr.

"Intellectual growth should commence at birth and cease only at death."
Albert Einstein

Do You Know?

Keeping your mind active and growing can have a significant effect on your quality of life as you age. It is true, "Use it or lose it."

Every day, there are about 500 books published in the U.S. (many hundreds more worldwide) and over one million new pages posted on the Internet.

Around the country and the world, there are low-cost lifelong learning opportunities. For example, some public colleges allow seniors to attend classes for free when space is available.

It has been said that the only difference between a rut and a grave is the dimensions.

What is "Growth?"

Keeping your mind active and growing can have a significant effect on your quality of life as you age. The National Institute on Aging funded research that has become known as "The Nun Study." The study, founded by principal researcher Dr. David Snowdon, began in 1986 and has followed the nuns at the convent of the School Sisters of Notre Dame in Minnesota.

The convent was chosen for the study because the environmental factors for the nuns were relatively constant. The nuns agreed to a number of study elements—to allow their early writings and biographies to be reviewed; to have their mental capacity tested periodically; and to have their brains autopsied when they died. One study conclusion has been that mental activity helps stave off degenerative brain diseases, like Alzheimer's. Remarkably, it also showed that some nuns whose autopsied brains showed that they, in fact, had Alzheimer's had not exhibited the symptoms of the disease (e.g., acute memory loss) when they were alive.

What have the researchers observed about why the nuns maintain their faculties as they age? There are a number of reasons, among them is that, through their faith, they have a sense of purpose. They also, in general, enjoy a quick sense of humor, teach and take classes on a variety of subjects, do crossword puzzles and read books, and focus on crafts hobbies. Said another way, they remain mentally active, and they continue to grow.

Growth is continuing to be mentally stimulated. As retirees, we should be familiar with the concept of growth, because that is what we experienced in our careers. Despite our level of education or chosen profession, we began our careers knowing little about how to really get things done. Through research, observation, trial and error, coaching from our superiors, mentoring from more experienced colleagues, and hard work, we grew in our jobs, hopefully, until we retired.

We also are familiar with growth with respect to our families. We began as novices when it came to creating a loving, nurturing marriage and rearing children. The same actions that helped grow our careers also helped grow our ability to build our families—research, observation, trial and error, coaching from our parents, mentoring from more experienced friends, and hard work.

As retirees, our careers are behind us, and while our families are still expanding as our children marry and grandchildren are born, most of our work is hopefully done. It is time for us to focus on growing ourselves in new dimensions. We were defined by where we worked and by our families. What will define us now, and how will we approach making progress in our new role? Thankfully, the actions required are what we are used to; research, observation, trial and error, coaching from expert resources, mentoring and learning the secrets from more experienced retirees, and hard work.

The risk of not growing is worse than maintaining the status quo; rather, it is losing ground. A lack of growth can result in boredom, unhappiness, depression, an earlier onset of dementia, and reduced longevity.

Many retirees report that they have not found a way to replace the intellectual stimulation that work afforded them. There are, however, many opportunities to stay mentally sharp and continue to grow. For example, retirees across the country and around the world are taking advantage of accessible and inexpensive lifelong learning opportunities to pursue new interests, enhance their knowledge about longtime passions, save money by learning "how to," build new social relationships, and simply foster their continued personal growth. The Osher Lifelong Learning Institute (OLLI), for example, has 121 locations at colleges and universities around the country. The Bernard Osher Foundation in San Francisco provides major funding. One of these programs is at the University of Cincinnati, which offers more than 100 courses each eight-week quarter. For a one-time $80 fee, you can attend as many of the courses, seminars, lectures, and field trips as you would like during that quarter. There are many other lifelong learning programs nationwide, including Institutes for Learning in Retirement (ILR), at numerous other U.S. colleges.

Mickey Sandmel, a secretary nearing retirement at a law firm, is a great example of planning for growth in the next phase of her life. She has always valued education, and after high school, while working fulltime and building a family, she persisted over 11 years to earn her degree in sociology. She instilled the importance of education in her three children, each who went on to earn degrees, including advanced degrees. Beginning in her 50s, Mickey began taking every course she could find time for, studying Russian, Spanish, Hebrew, and cooking. Now in her early 60s, Mickey has aspirations of returning to college to seek her Masters in an English-as-a-Second-Language program, a subject in which she has long been interested. Mickey's passion for education enables her continued personal growth.

Taking courses is but one way to personally grow. Take up a new sport. Volunteer for a meaningful cause. Visit a nearby museum. Write your memoirs. Play bridge. Do a crossword puzzle—or construct one. Do something new every day, regardless of how minor it might be. Drive a different route to the grocery store. Change the order of your morning routine. Get involved in activities that cause you to solve new problems; an approach that researchers have shown rewires the brain to build new capacity. Seek variety in your life; be curious; be spontaneous.

The good news is that there are innumerable activities that will foster positive change and progress in your life. More good news is that these activities need not be a chore, but are typically exciting and fun. Even more good news is that continuing to grow increases your mental energy, further building your capacity to live life to its fullest.

The final good news is that many of the best of these activities are, at most, a nominal cost.

A Flower over Her Ear

The remaining personal stories in this chapter are of people in their late-70s to mid-80s who are still very active and mentally sharp. Our intent in sharing these stories is not to imply that keeping yourself mentally stimulated and growing is only for octogenarians. Rather, it is to note that these role models established habits of engagement, curiosity, and interest early in their lives and sustained them over time. One good way to help ensure you sustain your mental energy is to create habits of continuous learning early in your life. The best time to start is now.

Vivian Kline was born in 1925 in an old brownstone house on the west side of Manhattan. Over the years, she married, moved to the Midwest, reared "three wonderful, successful and happy daughters," ran a co-op art gallery for more than two decades, retired, nurtured six grandchildren, has been active in political causes and for candidates, and enjoyed a 53-year enameling hobby.

Now in her mid-80s, Vivian remains vibrant, vital, interesting, interested, and involved. She plays tennis year-round, travels to visit family on both coasts, has replaced her creative enameling time with a new-found passion for writing poetry, continues to actively support her candidates and causes, and is a member of a writer's group that meets every Monday morning.

Vivian Kline with a flower over her ear

Vivian's energy and curiosity have enabled her to continue to grow, to keep her brain challenged and sharp. Some years ago, Vivian came across an old postcard, which referenced the Fisk University Jubilee Singers. She became interested in their history, researched it, and wrote, *Let Freedom Sing: Of 19th Century Americans: An Historical Novel or Could It Be a Musical?* She completed the book and published it at age 84, learning new things about writing, publishing, and herself along the way.

Vivian's energy is contagious. She lights up any room she is in with her smile and is always ready to share something she recently learned from her daily reading of the *New York Times* or from other sources. Vivian is a great storyteller, is a leader, has a great sense of humor, is still growing, and always wears a flower delicately placed over her right ear.

AGE

by Vivian B. Kline

You are as old as you feel
Though all has a beginning and an end.
Some cultures respect old age.
We try to deny it.
Body sculptors will tweak your shape
And earned wrinkles can be erased.

Yet houses very old are highly valued
And ancient trees are venerated.
Age used to be measured by rigid rules:
When boys should wear long pants
And girls put up their hair.
Now anything goes...or comes.

How old is old?
Do we need some markers?
Asians are one at birth.
Here: school at six; vote at eighteen;
Drink at twenty-five;
Medicare at sixty-five.

Remember old wood burns best;
Old wine preferred.
And ripe age gives tone to old violins.
With added years, a richer life begins:
The spirit mellows
And old friends become more valued.

Yet a crowded hour of glorious life
Is worth an old age without a name,
Don't you think?
We have played many parts along the way
And memories arise as time moves on.
A life well lived can be enjoyed again.

And you can be as young as you feel.

Use It or Lose It

There are many ways to ensure that you are continually expanding your horizons and keeping your mind sharp. Doing crossword puzzles is frequently given as but one example of how to challenge yourself and sustain your mental capacity. But, in the spirit of always looking for ways to add variety to your life, what if you are already doing crossword puzzles regularly? You can seek more difficult crosswords or add Sudoku or other puzzles or games to your repertoire.

There is another approach that can take puzzles to a new level. In late October 2009, this note accompanied the *New York Times* crossword puzzle, "All the daily crosswords this week...are by puzzlemakers who have been contributing to *The Times* for more than 50 years. Charles Gersch, of New York City, had his first crossword published on February 1, 1944, when he was 13, in the *New York Herald Tribune*."

Gersch, now in his late-70s, has, therefore, been constructing puzzles for over 65 years. Based on the complexity of his wide-open designs, one can see that puzzlemaking is his passion, has been fun, and has kept him sharp. Have you ever tried constructing a crossword puzzle? If words and puzzles are of interest to you, create your own puzzle, and you will see how mind-expanding it can be.

Lenora Sachar is in her mid-80s. About 1950, she began playing mah-jongg with 11 other women—enjoying the game, the challenge, and the social aspects of getting together with friends. Over the years, the group dwindled as members became ill or passed away. While Lenora still plays mah-jongg occasionally when she can find a game, she has switched her focus to playing bridge, beginning to learn the game when she was in her 60s and playing regularly ever since. She now plays three times per week with several different groups, again finding enjoyment in the game, the challenge, and the social aspects of getting together with friends.

Lenora Sachar

Lenora's activities are not limited to mah-jongg and bridge. She has volunteered at a local hospital and with an organization that conducts estate sales to raise money for a school that benefits children with multiple learning disabilities. She is an avid reader and is a member of a book club. Lenora does puzzles in the newspaper daily and is technologically ahead of many in her generation, in that she enjoys playing challenging games online.

Lenora has found games, books, and puzzles help keep her mentally sharp. She has also found that some of these activities have the social aspects she values so much and that help keep her young.

As noted earlier, we wanted to share examples of people who have continued to grow even into their later years, each having paid attention to being mentally stimulated earlier in life. Vivian, Charles, and Lenora are all great examples of the phrase, "Use it or lose it."

Key Learning about "Growth"

1. Staying intellectually stimulated by continuing to challenge yourself with new and interesting things will help ensure you maintain a high level of mental energy and capability as you age throughout your retirement years.
2. There are innumerable opportunities, both major and minor, to keep you mentally stimulated, bring variety to your life, and keep you learning. The opportunity is to take advantage of the ones that best suit you.
3. A significant proportion of growth opportunities require little or no financial investment.

Getting Started

1. Seek to experience something new in your life every day, whether it is a small or large change. Just as you diversify your financial portfolio, so should you diversify your life to stay sharp. The objective is to stay out of or get out of your rut and cause your brain to work.
2. Another way to get enhanced variety is to think about your routine. Areas of growth do not need to be brand new things, but can be extensions of what you already do. For example, if you enjoy reading history books, try reading novels. Listen to different music genres than you normally do. If you have an exercise routine, modify it, giving you both growth and well-being benefits.
3. Push yourself beyond your comfort zone. Take some risks on what you choose to do. If they do not work out, try something else. One of the joys of retirement is that you have time to make mistakes, learn from them, and move on. Each "failure" is a growth opportunity.

"Growth" Planning Worksheet

Personal Assessment: Rate the following statement from 1 to 5:
1 = This statement is far from describing activities that help me grow.
5 = This statement fully describes my activities that help me grow.

"My week is filled with new and challenging activities."

Rating: 1   2   3   4   5

Planning for "Growth"
What I will CONTINUE to do:

_____

_____

What I will START doing:

_____

_____

What I will STOP doing:

_____

_____

Other thoughts about Growth:

_____

_____

The one person in my life who can best help me to implement my immediate next step regarding Growth is

_____

_____

Chapter 15

Fun

*"Laughter is the shortest distance
between two people."*
Victor Borge

"If it's not fun, you're not doing it right."
Bob Basso

Do You Know?

Children laugh an average of 300 to 400 times each day while adults laugh an average of ten to 15 times each day.

Laughter improves the body's immune system, helping stave off the physical and emotional characteristics of chronic stress; has a positive effect on blood pressure and heart function; and it decreases pain. Socially, laughter strengthens relationships, helps reduce conflict, and promotes group bonding.

Men who have more orgasms not only are at a lower risk of contracting prostate cancer, but also have a significantly lower mortality rate. Sex is fun—right?

Having fun is intuitive, and we all want more of it. Why? We just do.

What is "Fun?"

Fun is one of those wonderful things that you will know when you see or feel it. Fun is enjoyment, pleasure, entertainment, merriment, and the opposite of boredom. Whether you are having fun when playing a sport, playing a board game, or playing with your grandchildren, you will know it. When you are having fun because you are deep into your hobby, you will know it. When you are having fun together with family or friends and laughing until your side splits, you will know it. When you are having fun learning something new and finding it fascinating, you will know it. When you are having fun doing something spontaneous, relishing the variety in your life, or quietly taking in the scenery around you, you will know it.

Similarly, you will know boredom when you see or feel it. When you have been watching television for hours a day, every day, you will know it. When you find yourself eating because you do not have anything else to do, you will know it. When you frequently get to the end of the day and are still in your pajamas (not a bad idea every once in awhile, but not frequently), you will know it. Friedrich Nietzsche, 19th century German philosopher, said, "Is not life a hundred times too short for us to bore ourselves."

Fun has a marvelous synergy within your retirement plan. It is likely as you choose activities that best fit the other key elements of a fulfilling retirement, most of them will be fun as well. Likewise, activities that you choose for fun will also be relevant to other key elements.

Have fun!

Just Do It

Fun has been defined as "something that provides amusement." "Hobby" has been defined as "an activity pursued for pleasure." Those sound pretty close, and, by most people's assessment, they are. Their hobbies are fun.

When David Nemon, who lives in Houston, Texas, was ten years old, his hobby was building model cars from kits—separating the pieces, fitting and gluing them together, and painting the chassis. When David's son was the same age, David tried to get him interested in model cars, but no deal. While he was exposing his son to his own boyhood hobby, David realized he missed the fun of creating the models. He renewed his hobby, and, now in his early 60s, David has been putting models together for years; mostly reissued models from the 50s and 60s. Cabinets in his home are full of completed cars.

David is playing with big cars also, having bought a restored classic two-door hardtop '57 Chevy. He only drives his non-air conditioned classic on the weekends to avoid heavy Houston traffic and in the winter to avoid heavy Houston heat and humidity.

Long-time retirees Sondi and John Davis share a golfing hobby. They not only play, but each year they take advantage of John's opportunity to volunteer at the Masters Golf Tournament in Augusta, Georgia, where Sondi enjoys spectating. Since retiring, Sondi and John, who also love to travel, have set the goal of playing golf in each of the 50 states and only have nine states to go, before they "start round two."

Barry Levin has lived all over the world as a diplomat for the United States State Department. Although Barry almost flunked high school French, he now finds languages challenging and fun. He speaks various levels of Japanese, Thai, Serbo-Croation, Greek, and French. As he approaches retirement, Barry is looking forward to the fun of learning Spanish.

Barry is also an avid guitarist, having first learned during high school. He even left college for a time to pursue his dream of becoming a rock star. Although that did not work out, Barry has continued to play in bands wherever he has lived and plans to continue playing in retirement.

Mike Fleischmann, a graphic designer for NBC's *TODAY* show, creates photos called "crossviews" and "anaglyphs" as a hobby. These are three-dimensional images created from photos taken with his digital camera. Mike takes a pair of shots slightly shifted laterally, and then processes them together. His fun is further enhanced as he sends his photos to those who share his hobby around the world. Mike is currently sharing with a fellow anaglyph hobbyist who lives in Rome. Mike, who is in his mid-60s, plans to carry his hobby into retirement.

Alan Resnick is retired from a career managing Landmark movie theaters in Los Angeles. For fun, Alan plays the guitar, listens to music, and revels in food—both cooking, which he has been studying for 25 years, and eating.

Gloria Scheinkman's hobby is her two bichon frise dogs, one who she breeds. Gloria also loves to bowl, do antiquing, and go to major league baseball games.

Arleen Bly sings and acts in local theater productions, plays mah-jongg and canasta with friends, reads voraciously, and dances every chance she gets.

Jill Chapin's hobby is words, so she spends time reading and writing. Her love of the language spills over to other pursuits; such as reading to second graders every week and watching them mesmerized by the story she is sharing with them.

Steve Karty—amateur radio

Judy Ellsley—dancing to the "oldies"

Allan Markovitz—his 2005 Harley Fat Boy motorcycle

Sherilyn and Barry Krell—visiting Presidential libraries

Debbie Pulley—gardening and decorating

Nancy Riesz—playing golf

Bob Miller—competitive rowing

Keith Lawrence—snowmobiling

Alan Spector—playing baseball

Marti Ferdman—book clubbing

Marla Levinson—yoga

You get the idea. The list of possibilities is endless. What is important is for you to discover a hobby (or two or three or…) that is fun for you and then, as Nike says, "Just do it."

Shapes in the Clouds

Hobbies are things we do for fun that tend to be structured activities. A less structured aspect of fun is spontaneity, something you do without planning or apparent cause, other than the opportunity to have fun.

Many of us were more spontaneous when we were younger. When Alan Spector's son, Kevin, was attending Washington University in St. Louis in the early 1990's, he called home one Monday to report that he had a wonderful time over the weekend at Mardi Gras in New Orleans. He had not planned to go to New Orleans, but on the previous Thursday evening, one of his fraternity brothers simply asked, "Who wants to go to Mardi Gras?" Twenty minutes later, Kevin and several others were in the car, and 700 miles later they were on Bourbon Street.

When Keith was driving his daughter, Jenny, to Indiana University, they saw an advertisement, and on the spur of the moment, decided to go skydiving. Jenny still talks about it as one of the most memorable times they had together.

When was the last time you did something like drive past a sign that said, "Introductory Soaring Lesson: $20," and stop to try it out?

When was the last time you were near a creek or pond and stopped to skip rocks?

When was the last time you decided on the spur of the moment to walk the two miles to a friend's house just to see if she was home?

When was the last time you were sitting at home at 8:00 on a Tuesday evening and said, "Let's go dancing?"

When was the last time you…?

Scott Adams, creator of *Dilbert*, wrote in his Blog, "As you know, you can fake most character traits if you need to. You can fake sincerity, kindness, compassion, optimism, and all sorts of things. But you can't fake spontaneity. I know because I've tried, and it always comes out sounding crazy. I'll blurt out something like 'Let's walk to Cuba,' and look at my wife to see if I nailed the spontaneous thing. So far, no luck. It's an elusive concept."

Marti Ferdman and her husband, Harvey, who you met in the "Well-Being" chapter, prefer driving to flying when they travel, because it allows them to be impulsive about changing their route. On a recent drive across Pennsylvania on their way back to the Midwest from visiting relatives in the Northeast, they made two unscheduled stops, one that had a serious bent, one that did not. They first saw a sign for Gravity Hill, near Paris, Pennsylvania, left the highway, and headed for the location where the sign claimed, "cars roll uphill and water flows the wrong way." They spent a couple of hours of fun enjoying rolling balls uphill and trying to figure out how the optical illusion worked.

After getting back on the highway, they soon realized they were in the area of Shanksville, Pennsylvania, and decided, on the spur of the moment, to visit the site of the September 11, 2001, plane crash. They also spent a couple of hours there, taking in the deep meaning and sorrow of the event and the location.

Back on the highway again and having spent a total of four hours at the two unplanned stops, Marti and Harvey did not feel as if they had wasted time on their trip. Rather, they felt that their lives had been enhanced by their spontaneity.

Their experience is reminiscent of the 1996 movie, *Michael*, in which an angel, played by John Travolta, asks the characters played by John Hurt, Andie MacDowell, and Robert Pastorelli to make stops on their car trip to see the world's biggest ball of twine and the world's largest non-stick frying pan.

Is a large ball of string, a hill that is an optical illusion, or the largest non-stick frying pan the most important thing in the world to see? No. Is doing things spontaneously fun? Yes. Is having fun an integral part of a fulfilling retirement? Yes. Is retirement a time in your life when you have the freedom to be spontaneous? Yes. It is the spontaneity and fun that make the event, the activity, the impulse.

There is another aspect to having fun that may not come foremost to mind. It is the fun that comes from simply enjoying the world around you. When you were a child, did you lie on your back on the lawn with a neighbor friend and try to find shapes in the clouds? Did you watch with wonder at a spider spinning a web? Did you search through a field of clover looking for that one elusive plant with four leaves? Did you catch lightning bugs, put them in a jar to see how they lit up your bedroom at night, and then release the bugs only to catch, perhaps, the same ones the next evening? Did you ever sit on your front porch and tingle with anticipation as a thunderstorm came across a field toward your house?

We would hope that in retrospect, you fondly recall those and similar childhood experiences as fun. Retirement gives you the opportunity and time to enjoy similar experiences.

Take a drive to the countryside and relish the starry sky. Visit a wildlife area, and just sit in the sunshine and watch the deer and birds. Be the first to leave footprints in fresh snow in an open field.

Oh, and, while you are at it, find shapes in the clouds, watch a spider spin a web, grab a jar and catch some lightning bugs, watch the thunderstorm approach, and find that four-leaf clover.

Key Learning about "Fun"

1. Having fun is a critical aspect of retirement. It is not only important in its own right, but it also helps you build stronger relationships, can improve your well-being, and offers many other intangible benefits.
2. Fun can be derived from many sources; for example, pursuing lifelong hobbies, laughing with friends, pausing to enjoy the beauty of the world that surrounds you, or doing something spontaneously.

Getting Started

1. Think about all the fun activities you have dreamed about over the years. You know which ones they are; the ones you have been putting off. Make your list and commit to do one or more of them

every couple of months.

2. Try different things, even if some stretch you out of your comfort zone. Recall Tim McGraw's hit song, "Live Like You Were Dying." Fun can be doing the big things in the song, like "Rocky Mountain climbing." Fun can also be the little things, like enjoying a floral display. Step out and go for it.

3. If there are distractions in your life that stand in the way of you having fun, such as daily chores or frustrating things you have been merely tolerating, identify them and put them on your worksheet list of things to stop. Do not let them drain the fun from your day.

"Fun" Planning Worksheet

Personal Assessment: Rate the following statement from 1 to 5:
1 = This statement is far from describing the level of fun in my life.
5 = This statement fully describes the level of fun in my life.

"I have many activities in my life that are just plain fun to do."

Rating: 1   2   3   4   5

Planning for "Fun"
What I will CONTINUE to do:

_____

_____

What I will START doing:

_____

_____

What I will STOP doing:

_____

_____

Other thoughts about Fun:

_____

_____

The one person in my life who can best help me to implement my immediate next step regarding Fun is

_____

Chapter 16

We're All in This Together

*"I think togetherness is a very important
ingredient to family life."*
Barbara Bush

*"Ideally, couples need three lives;
one for him, one for her,
and one for them together."*
Jacqueline Bisset

Do You Know?

Sixty percent of couples are not aligned about when each partner should retire. Nearly half do not agree on whether one or both partners should work in retirement. More than 40% do not agree on their expectations of lifestyle.

The second highest divorce rate is at 20 years of marriage when, in many cases, the children have grown, the couple has become "empty nesters," and they discover they are strangers.

Forty percent more people who are single are likely to be struggling in life than those who are married.

What is "We're All in This Together?"

Within several weeks, we each had the same conversation, but with different couples, each in which the husband had recently retired. Each of us asked the husband of a couple we know how his new retirement experience was going. Each husband smiled and said something like, "It is really going well; I've had time to completely reorganize the kitchen cabinets."

Shortly thereafter, each of us asked the wives how it was going now that their husbands had retired. They each responded with something like, "I can't wait until he finds another job or something else to do."

Elinore Miller Greenburg, EdD wrote an advice column for SilverPlanet.com, a web site for Baby Boomers and older readers. In mid-2008, a reader named Barbara wrote, "Dear Ellie, I have been retired for a few years and my husband just retired a few months ago. I can't believe how difficult it is having him home all the time. I can't get anything done. He's always in the way. I don't feel free to go out with my friends, to shop, or to go to meetings as I have done all during my married life, even when I was working. He's driving me crazy! What suggestions do you have?"

You are likely, in some way, in a close relationship. You may be married, living with a partner, close to your children, grandchildren or extended families or in any number of traditional or nontraditional relationships. Regardless of the association, your retirement will not only affect you personally, but those closest to you as well.

In the Appendix section entitled, "How to Use This Book," we suggest that there are options on how to do your planning if you are doing it with a partner or, perhaps, several family members. One option is for each partner to go through the process individually, then discuss your respective plans and modify them to meet the shared needs of the couple. The other option is to go through the process together, while being sensitive to the needs of the individuals. Regardless of which option you choose, you should end up with complementary individual plans.

Said simply, therefore, "We're All in This Together" is having a retirement plan that is yours and compatible with that of your planning partner(s).

Secret 7: Team Effort
- Your retirement affects those closest to you and making lasting change to get the most out of retirement requires their input and support.
- Identify, recruit, and involve your team; those who will help you on your quest.

Separate Computers

Steve and Janet Korach have settled into a fulfilling, balanced, and supportive retirement life. When Steve retired from a 32-plus year career a couple of years ago, he found the early months disorienting. Steve had thought through a plan for how he would utilize his time in retirement, but he did not feel it was coming together.

For one thing, Steve found himself imposing on Janet's space and time. He had spent more than three decades of 12-hour days and frequent business trips away from home. Now he was around the house seemingly all of the time. Janet had been a teacher early in their marriage, but left teaching to rear their children. With the children doing well and out on their own, Janet frequently tends to the grandchildren, plays golf, is the architect of their family tree, and pursues a passion for history as the curator of the local historic preservation association.

One seemingly trivial example of Steve and Janet figuring out how to share time and space during Steve's retirement was the availability of their one computer. While Steve was working and using his work computer, their home computer was Janet's virtually full time. With Steve at home, she would go to check e-mail or do something else and find him sitting there—at "her" computer. It took some time to figure out that a second system was needed. Looking back, Steve would have made sure a second computer was in the house before he retired. It turned out to be a less-than-trivial example.

The early bumps are well behind Janet and Steve. They are supportive of each other's individual plans and activities; working together to plan those things they will be doing together. This is really nothing new for them. During Steve's career, he had the opportunity to interview for a company position in Saudi Arabia, but before he even put his name in for the assignment, he and Janet spent days talking and thinking about all of the pros and cons. They made the decision together to go for the assignment, which Steve earned, and the Koraches spent two-plus years in Saudi Arabia.

Janet and Steve also worked closely together on his retirement decision. Janet suggested Steve consider retiring at age 55, because she knew that his job was stressful and thought he had earned retirement. Steve, however, did not feel ready. Although they were in a position to be financially secure, there were other considerations for Steve. He felt he still had contributions to make at work and still had the opportunity to grow personally by continuing on the job. He discussed this with his organization and was offered compelling projects that he envisioned taking another five years to adequately complete. He and Janet spent days talking and thinking about all of the implications. They made the decision together for Steve to continue working, and he continued to be energized by his work for another five years, eventually retiring just before his 60th birthday.

Building on their history of joint and thoughtful decision making, Janet and Steve learned to work through the early retirement time and space issues. They each have their full and fulfilling personal retirement plans and a shared plan for shared activities. They are also supportive of each other's individual pursuits.

Janet continues to spend time with grandchildren, volunteer, play golf, and pursue her historic preservation projects. Steve has found that he can select his retirement activities in a way that allows him to apply his skills, core values, and passions in the same way he did while working. Steve values faith, family, fitness, nurturing relationships, continual learning, and coaching others. To those ends, Steve is active in his Church, is the highest ranking volunteer of a local Boy Scout district that has 4200 boys and an organization of 30 volunteers reporting to him. He also plays golf regularly with a group of about 40 men and works out daily for an hour either at home or at the gym.

Janet and Steve Korach with Elijah,
the second of their three grandchildren

Janet and Steve spend a considerable amount of time together taking care of their three grandchildren, playing golf, and enjoying trips to their timeshares in Florida and Hawaii, where they were once stationed when Steve was in the service. They also make decisions together that affect both of them—talking and thinking about the pros and cons, then deciding together. They even work on their separate computers—together.

Different Journeys

Trish Martindell and her husband, Jack, go their own way each day and may see each other about 5:00pm each afternoon. They retired about the same time, Jack in September 2001 and Trish in July 2002, yet their individual retirement journeys have been very different. They are developing a shared journey as well.

Shortly before Trish retired, she moved her father from his home in Arizona to a nursing home near her. About six months after Trish's mother died, her father began a quick decline into dementia and needed additional care and her involvement. When she retired, Trish began spending late afternoon-early evening time with her father every day and did so for four years until he passed away—being grateful for every day she had with him.

There were other things that occupied her early retirement as well. She took courses in pottery making and tax preparation, seemingly disparate activities, but consistent with earlier interests. Trish has always loved crafts, had enjoyed discovering and purchasing pottery over the years, finally deciding to create pieces herself. It has become a full-blown passion, and she gets great joy from fashioning pottery for friends and family, as well as selling some pieces.

During her work life, for a brief time before she became a corporate Information Technology Manager, Trish had done tax preparation for H&R Block and loved it. When she retired, she took the requisite classes to get back into the field, wanting the enjoyment of doing the work and of helping people at the same time. She spent each of her first five retirement winters preparing taxes in a CPA office.

Trish also spent the first 18 months of retirement trying to keep her calendar as full as it was when she was working. She joined a golf league and a bowling league and was meeting friends most days for lunch. This was in addition to her work on the boards of two non-profits, working out three times per week, her pottery, her tax work, and visiting with her father. She was always busy, and it took her those first months to figure out that being busy was not the objective. She needed more balance in her life. Trish finally settled into a comfortable rhythm of activity and leisure. She is still busy, but not overly so.

Trish has also found out a lot about herself in retirement.

When she was working, the demands of her job made every day very different. There was little risk of the job becoming routine. Her retirement activities, however, while energizing to begin with, have become routine for Trish over time, causing her to reevaluate each of them. She left her tax preparation work when it became routine. She takes a break from pottery every so often. And she continues to look for new opportunities. Trish has learned it is time for her to renew her retirement plan when she loses energy, feels bored, and is not learning anything new.

Jack and Trish Martindell

Jack's journey has been the inverse of Trish's. Jack spent the first couple of years of retirement doing the manual labor of rehabbing older homes to resell them. While doing so was satisfying on one level, Jack had two issues with this work: 1) it was not mentally stimulating, and 2) he hurt his back and was unable to continue. He became disenchanted with retirement, seldom had anything to do, and found it difficult to develop an interest. For awhile, he even stopped trying. Fortunately, for his health and Trish's peace of mind, Jack began to find his way.

During his career years, Jack had enjoyed the outside activity of being involved in city politics, acting as campaign manager for a mayoral candidate. Jack was contacted by a local politician who remembered Jack's work on the previous campaign. He was back in politics, both working on campaigns and getting involved with his party's organization. While Jack had stayed involved with building rehab by hiring others to do the manual labor, it was the return to politics that rejuvenated him. He has now become involved in other things, including non-profit Board work.

Taking different paths, Trish and Jack have developed full and fulfilling individual retirement lives. In addition, they have set out on a new adventure together. They are empty nesters for the first time, but did not become so in the conventional sense. Their children have been out of the home for some time, but the Martindells had continued to keep pets. Recently, however, the family cat died after long bouts with illnesses that made it difficult for Trish and Jack to leave home for any length of time. For the first time ever, they have no at-home responsibilities other than themselves. This has given them the freedom and flexibility to do the traveling they have wanted to do for some time. They are also discussing whether or not to spend their winters in warmer climes.

The Martindells' retirement lives are driven mostly by their individual interests and plans, but empty nesting is increasing their time together. Travel and other shared activities are now being woven into their individual and collective lives. Trish and Jack's retirement journeys have been different from each other's and different from yours and mine. What is important is that each of them individually has and the two of them together have achieved increased fulfillment.

It is important that you do the same. It is likewise important that like the Koraches and the Martindells, you share and plan with partners and other family members who will be affected by your retirement and the choices you make; the earlier the better.

Key Learning about "We're All in This Together"

1. Your retirement affects not only you but also your family and friends.
2. The most successful retirements are those in which the individual and shared plans of partners are compatible with each other.
3. It is best to discuss and develop retirement plans together proactively instead of reactively.

Getting Started

1. Involve those who will be impacted by your retirement planning early in your thinking. Get their input on each of the key elements of a fulfilling retirement. You will not only get great ideas that will result in a better plan for you, but also build more compatibility among your individual and shared plans.

2. If your partner has not gone through this book with you, be sensitive to the fact that he or she does not have the same level of knowledge you do. You may want to encourage your partner to read the book as well.

3. Recognize you are entering a new daily routine in your home. Have a discussion with your partner about how that daily routine will work and who will have responsibility for what. It is better to have this discussion early instead of waiting until you realize you need to have it.

"We're All in This Together"
Planning Worksheet

Personal Assessment: Rate the following statement from 1 to 5:
1 = This statement in no way describes my retirement plan.
5 = This statement fully describes my retirement plan.

"My retirement plan takes into account the needs of my partner and any affected family and friends."

Rating: 1 2 3 4 5

Planning for "We're All in This Together"
Who are the people in my life I will involve as I develop my plan?

_____

_____

_____

How might my retirement affect others?

_____

_____

_____

Other thoughts about "We're All in This Together":

_____

_____

The one person in my life who can best help me to implement my immediate next step regarding "We're All in This Together" is

_____

Chapter 17

Making Choices

—

Establishing Your Plan

*"It is never too late to be
what you might have been."*
George Eliot

*"Organizing is what you do
before you do something,
so when you do it,
it is not all mixed up."*
A. A. Milne

Do You Know?

Eighty-three percent of people do not have clearly defined goals. Fourteen percent have goals, but they are not written down. The remaining 3% that have written goals and a plan earn, on average, 10 times more.

Many of us hesitate to make decisions and, therefore, do not choose to make the beneficial changes in our lives to reach our full potential.

Having a plan helps you get clear about what you want to do, and writing it down helps you hold yourself accountable to do it.

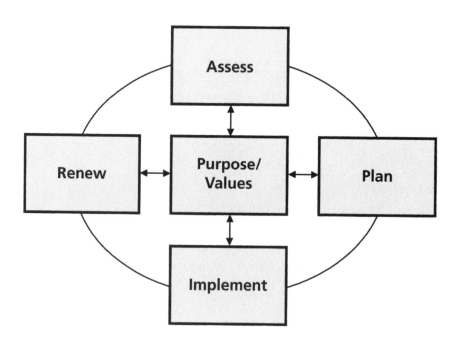

What is "Making Choices— Establishing Your Plan?"

Through the book, you have made progress using the planning model. You have learned more about your life purpose and personal values. Using the planning worksheets, you have done an assessment of where you currently rate yourself for each of the key elements. You have identified and charted activities in the Start, Stop, and Continue sections of the worksheets. You are well prepared for the focus of this chapter, which is the "Plan" block on the model.

In that regard, "Making Choices—Establishing Your Plan" means considering your options and making the choices that will comprise your plan. Once you have your plan in place, you will move on in subsequent chapters to putting your plan into action ("Implement") and eventually, to keeping your plan fresh over time ("Renew").

Each of us has a different approach to making decisions and planning. Some of us are highly organized; others are more spontaneous. Some of us are very rigorous decision makers and planners; others less so. Some of us are written list makers; others have a mental list or take things as they come. While we are sensitive to these differences, our intent is to share with you what are some of the best-known ways to help you successfully make choices to build your plan, a critical step on the way to having a fulfilling retirement. One piece of guidance stands out at this point; when you make choices to create your plan, write them down. Be one of the 3% who do this!

What you will have at the end of this chapter is a personal plan, unique to you and your circumstances. You will get there by first thinking about the choices you will make, then building those choices into a plan.

Seashells

Our basic premise is that your best choices will be those that have a positive effect on multiple key elements. These holistic choices will enable you to make the most of your time, energy, and talents and have the most positive impact on your retirement life.

Diane and Terry Batsch are a great example of making holistic choices. Diane and Terry are in their mid-60s and have been retired for a decade. They make an annual pilgrimage to Florida each February to get a break from the winter cold. A favorite Florida pastime has been to leisurely walk the beach, collecting a wide variety of shells. For many years, Diane and Terry would collect, clean, and dry hundreds of shells, displaying some in their home, giving some to grandchildren, and storing the remainder.

Diane and Terry Batsch with their Seashells book

One year Terry had an idea that added meaning to their pleasant pastime. Diane's sister is an inner-city elementary school teacher in Minneapolis. It struck Terry that most if not all of his sister-in-law's students had never seen a beach, and many might never get to a beach in their lifetimes.

What if he could develop a lesson plan for the class based on the seashells? Terry began studying sea life and their shells, finding ways to describe them to students. With the lesson plan complete, he filled plastic bags, each one containing 12 to 15 different shells—enough bags for each student to have his or her own. It was time to run an experiment.

Terry received enthusiastic support from a local inner city school administration and conducted his first class. Terry beams as he describes how energized the children were by the lesson, how they chattered with delight and pride as they identified their shells, and how they squealed with joy when he told them they would get to keep their bags of shells and take them home.

With the experiment a success, Terry sent his lesson plan and sufficient shell bags to his sister-in-law. She conducted the lesson and had the same exciting success. Each year, Terry teaches the lesson at the original school, sends shell bags to his sister-in-law, and has added his grandchildren's schools to his teaching schedule.

One of the most rewarding aspects of the program is the packets of individually handwritten thank you notes the Batsches routinely receive from the children. The children's simple expression of thanks and unique descriptions of their favorite shells are entertaining and immensely gratifying.

Diane and Terry continue to travel to Florida each February, continue to leisurely walk the beach collecting shells, and continue to clean and dry them. They have now, however, added the new dimensions to their holistic retirement plan. They are giving back and making a difference in the lives of young people. Terry is connected to the schools and the children, many of whom he will never meet. Diane and Terry have experienced personal growth, because they have continued to study the sea life that is the basis for their new-found activity. To top it off, what started as fun is now even more so.

Diane and Terry have a more meaningful and holistic retirement plan.

Finding Your Seashells

As you make your planning choices, you will be answering many of the key questions most retirees have. How will I spend my time? What will I do to replace the intellectual stimulation, daily structure, relationships, and sense of purpose that I have or had in the workplace? How will I redefine myself in retirement? How can I make the many choices in front of me? How can I take advantage of all of the opportunities?

Our suggested approach to answering most retirement questions is to look at the question holistically, in a way that takes all of the key elements into account. It is on this basis that we will guide you through an approach to putting your plan together. Let us look at an example of a question we frequently hear, "Should I be working after I retire?"

This is a great question, especially considering two sets of facts. First, the 2006 Merrill Lynch New Retirement Survey showed that 71% of Baby Boomers anticipate working in some capacity in retirement; two-thirds of those in different kinds of jobs than those of their primary career. Second, while it may be difficult to believe so in the current job market, some estimates indicate that there will be a labor shortage in the United States before 2020. Many of these jobs will be in the social sector, including health, education, government, and non-profits. It would not be surprising if supply and demand brought baby boomer retirees and work opportunities together in some capacity.

While the question of whether or not to work in retirement seems relatively straightforward, there are many factors to consider:

- Do I need to earn money or receive health insurance benefits to ensure my financial security once I am no longer in my primary career? (Financial Security)
- Should I find a part-time job to help replace some of the things my career provided me—camaraderie, intellectual stimulation, a sense of purpose? (Connectedness, Growth, Purpose/Values)
- Will a part-time job help ease my transition from working full time into the new phase of my life? (Stages of Retirement)
- Is there a job that I should be doing that better matches the things I am passionate about? (Passions)
- Would it be best for me to be spending my time working versus volunteering? (Giving Back)
- What impact might working have on others in my life? (Connectedness)

As noted, these questions relate to many of the key elements of a fulfilling retirement. The answer to "Should I be working after I retire?" can be best answered, therefore, by holistically considering the effect on each of the key elements. Just as Diane and Terry Batsch chose their seashell activity that positively affected so many of the key elements, so can you make decisions holistically.

While it may not seem so initially, the working-in-retirement question is similar to the question, "Where should I live when I retire?" What is the similarity? This is another example of an important question that can best be answered by holistically considering multiple key elements. With regards to the location choice, here is a sampling of considerations:

- Do I need to reduce my living expenses to be financially secure? For example, should I downsize from my home to a smaller condominium? Should I move from the expensive city where I live to one with a lower cost of living? Should I sell my house and choose to rent? (Financial Security)
- Do I want to be closer to family or friends to be more connected? For example, should I move to be closer to my grandchildren? Should I move to be closer to my aging and ailing parents to provide them the support they need? (Connectedness)
- Do I need to change location for health and well-being reasons? For example, should I move to a warmer climate where it is easier to stay active and fit? (Well-Being)
- Should I move to a location that allows me to more readily pursue my passions? For example, should I move to a lake community because I love boating? Should I move to Florida to be able to play golf year-round? Should I live part of the year in one location and part in another to meet my needs? (Passions)

The working in retirement and location questions are but two examples of the choices you have in front of you. With your knowledge of the key elements, you will find you will be able to readily sort through opportunities to consider your options holistically and, as a result, make better choices.

Making Your Right Choices

You may be able to make the choices about what you want in your plan without a structured approach. If however, you find you are having difficulty sorting through all of your options, using the following structure may be helpful to you. Even if you do not actually complete the recommended chart, the concepts it uses should be useful. This approach will give you the insight you need to actually "make a call" and add confidence to act on your choices.

The approach takes advantage of your new-found understanding of the key elements. List them down one side of a piece of paper or format a chart on your computer, similar to what we have done in the chart below.

Activities	Activity A	Activity B	Activity C
Key Elements			
Purpose/Values			
Attitude			
Well-Being			
Financial Security			
Connectedness			
Giving Back			
Passions			
Growth			
Fun			
Total			

Recall, you have been accumulating potential activities on the worksheets in the earlier chapters. Use those worksheets to write the possible activities across the top of the chart, similar to what we have done with Activities A, B, and C. You will need more room than our chart provides, because you will have more than a few activities from which to choose. You may want to take some time to research what other activities you might consider. Talk to friends and family or search for other resources. It may also be worthwhile for you to seek out an expert, like a life coach or a career counselor, depending on your individual needs.

Once your chart is constructed, go activity by activity and put a plus sign (+) in the cell for every key element the activity might positively affect. If you believe an activity could be of extraordinary benefit for a key element, put in two pluses (++). If you believe an activity has a negative effect on a key element, put a negative sign (-) next to the key element for that activity. Similarly, use a double negative, if appropriate (--). If the activity seems to have no effect on a key element, leave that cell blank. Here are some examples of how activities might affect key elements:

- If you are considering a volunteer activity at your church, this should positively affect "Giving Back." (Put a + in that cell under the volunteer activity.)
- If you are considering beginning a course at a local University, this should positively affect "Growth." (Put a + in that cell under the course activity.)
- If you choose to start a well-designed, thorough exercise program with a personal trainer, "Well-Being" is positively affected (+). If you are starting from a situation in which you have not exercised for some time, you may consider the activity as having an increased positive effect, warranting a double-plus (++).
- Each activity will likely affect more than one key element. For example, you may be considering writing a book. You might judge this to have a positive effect on your "Growth" (+), but a negative effect on "Connectedness" (-) if you view doing so as a solitary endeavor that will limit your time with friends and family.

Take the time to do this thorough analysis for each activity. Doing so should not be a burdensome exercise. Go through and make judgments quickly, using your intuition. Spending inordinate time agonizing over every cell will not add value to your analysis and will likely become a barrier to you taking full advantage of this approach. You will find your first instincts will work for you, but you can also revisit your analysis later if it is helpful to do so.

What you will have in front of you when it is complete is a picture of your decision making information. You will see that some activities are heavy with pluses; some have a single plus and perhaps a minus; others more balanced. The chart will not make the decision for you, but it will give you a good view of which activities will have the most holistic and, therefore, high-leverage impact on the meaningfulness of your retirement life.

You may even want to add a row at the bottom, as we have in our chart above, that allows you to total your pluses and minuses. Add your number of pluses in each activity column, subtract the number of minuses, and write down the resulting number. The activities with the highest numbers may be those you choose to pursue.

There are, however, other factors to be considered when making your choices:

- You may have identified so many great activities that there are not enough hours in the day to begin them all now. You will need to set priorities, and we will also address this in more detail later in this chapter and in "Doing What You Planned."

- You may find some undertakings, like deciding to move to Florida, to be too big to jump into. Rather, you might want to find ways to experiment with them before taking the plunge. To follow the Florida example, spend a month in the area you are interested in to get a feel for whether the choice will give you the benefits you envision. You will see more about this concept of "practicing retirement" in "Doing What You Planned."

- You may make choices that affect your spouse, partner, family members, or friends. The implications of this and how to address them was covered in more detail in Chapter 16, "We're All in This Together."

- You should consider the future implications of your choices that are beyond near-term activities. For example, you might decide to permanently move to a location that gets you out of the winter cold. As you grow older, however, you might find that this choice moved you farther from family that could provide needed support. If you perceive this could be an issue for you, you might want to find a different way to beat the cold, like keeping your current home and visiting the warmer climes only in winter.

- Finally, you may have special considerations that affect the choices you can make. These circumstances may change what you are able to do, because of their effect on your time, energy, and resources. Just a few of the many possible examples are the following: your daughter, son-in-law, and their baby have moved back in with you for an indeterminate period while they work through a difficult economic time; you are a single grandparent and are raising your grandchild; your elderly father needs ever-increasing support, and you are his only child living nearby; you injured your back and are going through rehabilitation, uncertain of the eventual outcome. We will address these special considerations later in this chapter.

Putting It All Together

It is time to put all of your learning and introspection together. It is time to make your choices and develop your first written plan. There are several points to review. You will be utilizing the key elements/activities chart from earlier in the chapter; if you have not yet filled it out, you may want to do so at this time.

Recall that you will likely want to make activity choices to yield the most holistic effect. On your chart, your most holistic activities will be those with the greatest number of pluses and the least amount of minuses; resulting in the highest numbers in the bottom row.

Also recall that if you have a partner that will be affected by your retirement plan, or yours by him or her, determine how you want to involve him or her (or them) in your decision making. Depending on how you have chosen to integrate your partner into your planning and decision making, this may be the time to get him or her involved.

In a perfect world with infinite time, energy, and resources, you would, perhaps, choose to do all of the activities listed across the top of your chart. However, given finite time, energy, and resources and given the necessity to also do the chores of daily life and tend to special considerations (more about both of these shortly), you will need to make some priority decisions. One priority decision will be which activities to put in your plan (Start or Continue). Even choosing to Stop an activity may take some effort, though it should eventually free up time and energy. The other priority decision will be which activity or activities to get started on first.

When we suggested in the Worksheet Instructions that you circle those "...one or two activities that you will likely want to act on immediately...," we were jumpstarting your priority setting process. In that regard, your worksheets will be a resource to you as you both choose activities and set priorities. There will be more about setting priorities later in the chapter.

We will add one simple, yet important chart, before you get started. The Start/Stop/Continue chart is where you will write down the activity choices and when you plan to begin each one. In essence, the chart will become your plan.

You may find you need fewer or more than the four activity spaces we have provided in each of the categories, Start, Stop, or Continue. If you need more space, use extra paper or format your own chart on the computer. You can also use the forms you'll find at www.YourRetirementQuest.com to write down your plan. Recognize, however that your plan will change over time and you will need a place to capture those changes.

		Activities	Start Date
Start	1.		
	2.		
	3.		
	4.		
Stop	1.		
	2.		
	3.		
	4.		
Continue	1.		
	2.		
	3.		
	4.		

Chart Example/How to Write Activities

Before you complete your chart, we would like to share an example of a completed chart with you and to discuss how to best word your activity choices. In Chapter 6, Alan shared his retirement planning story with you. We are going to use his story as an example to create a chart for you. The following was Alan's plan in January 2002, just before he retired that May. It is different than the plan he had when Ann and he began planning for and practicing retirement five years earlier and has changed many times since as Alan has continued to renew the plan. Like any plan, therefore, it was merely a snapshot of that point in time.

Plan (1/02)	Activities	Start Date
Start	1. Obtain Personal Trainer certification and research opportunities for giving back by volunteering personal training time to seniors.	7/02
	2. Analyze spending each month versus our retirement budget.	2/02
	3. Build stronger connections with high school classmates.	5/02
	4. Construct crossword puzzles with the objective of eventually having some published.	1/03
	5. Increase amount of leisure reading with a focus on mysteries.	5/02
Stop	1. Family tree development for my family to support Ann's work on her father's family tree.	2/02
	2. Doing my own yard work.	4/02
Continue	1. Play baseball in local leagues, and in tournaments around the country and the world. Add a tournament in Cooperstown.	ongoing
	2. Conduct financial advisor quarterly reviews.	ongoing
	3. Schedule weekly physical training visits to the gym 4 to 6 days each week.	ongoing
	4. Complete newspaper puzzle page daily.	ongoing
	5. Visit family in St. Louis and in Northeast frequently.	next-3/02

There are some things you may note about the choices in this plan:

- The overall plan is holistic in that it affects each of the key elements of a fulfilling retirement.

- Many of the individual activities are holistic in that they affect multiple key elements. An example is the first Start activity. Obtaining the Personal Trainer certification will require keeping physically fit (Well-Being), while learning new things (Growth). Once the certificate is earned, it will lead to volunteering time to seniors who need the service but cannot afford it (Giving Back) and building relationships with individual clients and exercise classes (Connectedness). On top of that, because Alan enjoys physical training, the activity will be Fun.

- Each activity is written with some specificity; describing not only what Alan is intending to do, but also when and how much or how often. As examples: daily puzzle pages, quarterly reviews with Financial Advisors, monthly spending reviews, adding a specific baseball tournament. This kind of specificity will help you take the next step to implement the activity and help you put events on your calendar or to-do list to make sure they are scheduled.

- There are two Stop activities. It is sometimes hard to identify what you will not do. You can become overcome by inertia. When you originally started something, you did it for a reason, and subsequently choosing to stop it later might make you feel uncomfortable. The questions, however, are what are the priorities in your life and what are the things that are getting in your way of creating the fulfilling retirement you want. Alan enjoyed working on his family tree, but helping Ann with hers meant spending more time with her and learning more about how to do it well, so he could be more successful later. Alan also enjoyed mowing the grass and working in the yard. However, when he compared doing that to the many other things of interest to him, he made a choice to give up yard work.

Daily Routine/Special Considerations

As you consider the key element activity choices for your plan, it will be important to understand how much time each activity will take and its priority. Recognize that your time and priorities are also affected by your chores of daily living and those things in your life that are special considerations.

The chores of daily living, as you know, make up a long list—

from grocery shopping to getting a haircut; from doing the laundry to mowing the lawn; from cooking dinner to making the bed; and everything in between. Peter Graham, now in his early 70s, recalls early in his retirement that he and his wife needed to get clear on who would get the mail each day or answer the phone at home when it rang. While small tasks, they are not trivial and must be done.

We suggest you take daily living tasks into account as you develop your plan. We further suggest that you not write down all these important yet routine activities. Writing down "continue to brush my teeth" or "continue to get dressed in the morning" is clearly unnecessary and would overwhelm the important things in your plan you want to change in your life. That being said, one of the things you should notice over time is that daily chores are a prime target for an exercise to declutter and simplify your life to make room for more fulfilling activities. It will be helpful to answer the question, "What are the things I am doing routinely that do not need to be done, can be done more efficiently, or can be done by others to free up my precious time?"

One other point about daily chores; you may find that some things that you consider chores while you are working may show up differently to you when you have more time to give to them. An example is cooking. When you are working, preparing meals may be viewed as something during your day that needs to be done, but for which you have too little time. When you are retired, you may find that cooking is something you enjoy, because when you can spend more time with it, it is enjoyable and, perhaps, even a hobby. We know several retirees who have discovered cooking is a passion and are loving it. A similar transition can take place from mowing the lawn, perhaps a time-consuming nuisance while you are working, to landscaping your property, a creative outlet when you are retired. If you find these shifts from chores to valued activities occur, write them down in your plan.

Special considerations, many of which are family obligations, may also take a significant portion of your time, energy, and resources. These considerations will change throughout your retirement. Examples we shared earlier are these: your daughter, son-in-law, and their baby have moved back in with you for an indeterminate period while they work through a difficult economic time; you are a single grandparent rearing your grandchild; your elderly father needs ever-increasing support, and you are his only child living nearby; you injured your back and are going through rehabilitation, uncertain of the eventual outcome.

In the last chapter, you met Trish Martindell, who spent several hours each day for four years with her father in the dementia unit of his care facility. While she was saddened by his decline and despite the time she dedicated to him, Trish was glad for every moment she had with her father—he was a very special consideration in her life.

Once you are confronted with and accept the special consideration, it becomes part of your life plan and must be taken into account. These circumstances are substantial and changing over time. We, therefore, suggest you write them down—add them to your chart.

Now you are ready to take some quiet time to fill out your plan. Use your worksheets and activities/key elements chart to help make your choices and set your priorities. Be specific about your activity wording. Create holistic activities and an overall holistic plan. Establish a time you plan to get started. Include your special considerations. These are the activities that you believe you want to Start, Stop, or Continue to move you toward a more fulfilling retirement.

Priority Setting

Now that you have your Start/Stop/Continue planning chart filled out, it is time to review it in its entirety. Your objective is to have a plan that feels as though it will guide you to live a full and fulfilling retirement life without being overwhelming. You want to be busy with meaningful things to do, but not so busy that you feel beleaguered. You want to balance busy-ness with leisure, good stress with relaxation, challenge with comfort, and stimulation with recovery time.

If the plan feels like it may be too much to take on, there are two possibilities. One is that you are right and you should pare it down. The other is that you may not yet be good at judging your retirement rhythm. If that is the case, you may find that what looks too big might be just right or, perhaps, even undersized. We do not want you to be discouraged by trying to take on a plan that cannot be successful, yet we also believe you may surprise yourself by being able to pull it off and by enjoying the satisfaction of doing so.

One way to deal with a plan with many activities is to set priorities. You only need to do this if you are concerned about not being able to do everything. For activities you want to start, try using this simple system by going through each activity and assign an A, B, or C to each.

"A" – activities you must do to feel you are fully living your life's purpose; they are extremely important to you, and you must do them to ensure a fulfilling retirement

"B" – activities that are important to you and you want to do them, but are not essential to fulfilling your life purpose

"C" – activities that would not leave you with regrets were you to not do them; they are of lesser importance and would be nice to do if time permits

Once you have assigned the letters, you can then determine when to take the steps you need to get the activities started, beginning with A, then B, then C. You will want to eventually begin all of them, but separating them by time may make that easier.

For activities you are continuing, this should not be an issue. For those you wish to stop, decide when to do that in the context of the other parts of your plan and depending on how difficult it might be to stop the activity.

Recall also, that in retirement, you are the boss. If you get started and the plan is not doable, change it. Remember, "A plan is only something from which to deviate." We will discuss this further in Chapter 19, "Renewing Your Plan."

You have chosen your list of activities based on knowledge, introspection, and intuition. Go with your gut and give it a try. Mark Twain said, "Twenty years from now you will be more disappointed by the things you didn't do than by the ones you did do. So throw off the bowlines. Sail away from safe harbor. Catch the trade winds in your sail. Explore. Dream. Discover."

Key Learning about "Making Choices— Establishing Your Plan"

1. Choose activities that positively affect multiple key elements thereby resulting in a holistic and more successful plan.
2. Retirement is a learning journey; you can try activities that intrigue you and not worry if they do not work out perfectly for you. These activities teach you more about what is important to you.
3. Having a plan, preferably written, is an important step to take toward a successful retirement. The plan helps you get clear on what you want to do, and writing it down helps you hold yourself accountable to do it.

Getting Started

1. Do two things with your completed plan:
   a. Evaluate your plan on your own to confirm that it feels balanced, energizing, and doable to you.
   b. Share your draft with a family member or close friend. You may also find it worthwhile to share it with a recognized expert, like a life coach or a career counselor, whoever can bring the best expertise to helping you evaluate your particular plan.
2. If you found you had difficulty making choices to develop your plan, take a quiet moment to jot down what you believe is getting in your way. Perhaps you have some fears about retirement and concerns about making the choices. Talk over these potential impediments with someone with whom you are comfortable discussing the obstacles. You may want to prompt the discussion by asking, "How real are my concerns?" or "What is the worst that can happen if I make some choices?" You may also consider contacting a LifeScape, LLC coach at www.LifeScapeRetirement.com.
3. Write down what you learned about yourself and how you make decisions. These thoughts may help you as you proceed to implement and, eventually, renew your plan. Use the worksheet on the next page to capture your thoughts.

"Making Choices—Establishing Your Plan" Planning Worksheet

Personal Assessment: Rate the following statement from 1 to 5:
1 = This does not exist in my life today.
5 = I have this completely covered.

"I have a plan for my retirement. It is written down and up to date."

Rating: 1   2   3   4   5
(before completing this chapter)

Rating: 1   2   3   4   5
(after completing this chapter)

Thoughts about "Making Choices—Establishing Your Plan":

_____

_____

_____

_____

_____

_____

_____

The one person in my life who can best help me with Making Choices—Establishing My Plan is

_____

Enjoy The Rewards

In the first section of the book, you began to envision *Your Retirement Quest*. In the second section, you developed a retirement plan you can embrace. You know, therefore, where you are going and what you want to do to get there. This book section will enable you to enjoy the rewards of your quest by bringing your plan to reality and keeping it fresh through the years.

Chapter 18 will give you a framework, based on the best known approach, to implement your plan successfully and fulfill the challenge we posed in Chapter 1. "Doing What You Planned" explains how the concepts of Skill, Will, and Support will help you implement your plan.

You have been reading about people who began to experiment with their retirement activities while they were still working. If you have yet to retire, we will be more specific in this section about the concept of "practicing retirement."

As you age through your retirement journey, life circumstances will change and new opportunities will present themselves. Some of the changes and the opportunities will be good; others will be traumatic. In either case, "Renewing Your Plan" and being resilient to adapt to the new conditions will be crucial to continuing to live a full and fulfilling retirement.

Having developed your plan and learned strategies to implement it and keep it fresh, you will enter the final chapter of the book ready to be "Living Fully."

Chapter 18

Doing What You Planned

"Thinking well is wise; planning well, wiser;
doing well is wisest and best of all."
Persian Proverb

"Sometimes you just have to take the leap and
build your wings on the way down."
Kobi Yamada

Do You Know?

Only 20% of those who have experienced heart attacks, a population that should be well-motivated to alter their behavior, make sustained behavioral changes.

Less than 10% of all New Year's resolutions become reality.

A common denominator among those who successfully change their lives is having someone to help them be accountable for the change.

Despite the difficulty of making sustainable change, doing so is possible, and the benefits are worth it.

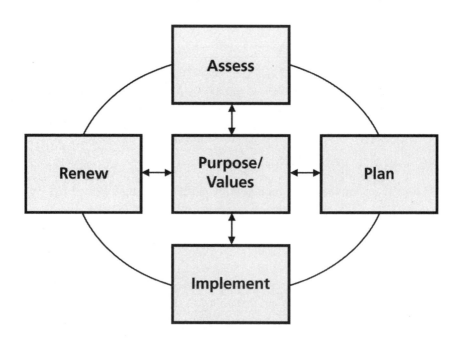

What is "Doing What You Planned?"

In Chapter 1, "Get Serious about Your Retirement," we extended a challenge to you. That challenge was to *understand what it takes to make a change in your life and beat the odds, so that you will be able to create a better retirement life for yourself*. In this chapter, we will share with you concepts and approaches that will help you be among those who can and do make a difference in their lives.

You have taken the first step already; you have a plan. You are now ready to be in the "Implement" block of the model.

Some call it "implementation;" some call it "execution;" some call it "delivering on the promise." Regardless of what you call it, the intent is to do what you planned to do. Social scientists and business consultants who have studied this area refer to it as the technology of "change management." There are some key principles and guidelines that support change management.

1. Be selective and specific about what you are intending to do. This is what you already did when you created your plan. In essence, your plan is a commitment to yourself. For example, suppose, as one of your Start activities, you wrote, "I will spend 30 minutes meditating every morning."

2. Assess whether you have the capability, the "Skill," to do what you have chosen. If not, a first step will be to learn more about how to do the activity. In our example, you might say, "I don't know how to meditate, so I will read a book about meditation and take a course at the local recreation center."

3. Link your new behavior to your life purpose or a core value, a step that helps ensure you have the motivation or "Will" to make the change. In our example, a key value for you may be "the importance of family." The link between the action and your key value would cause you to say, "I am planning to meditate regularly, so that I will be calmer and more patient with my grandchildren."

4. Surround yourself with an environment to "Support" what you want to do; making it more likely that you will do your activity than not do it. "I will arrange a section of my spare bedroom to have the peace and quiet I need for my meditation."

5. Identify and recruit an accountability partner. Perhaps you have a friend with whom you go to the gym. Ask her if every Friday, before you begin your workout, she will ask you, "How many times have you meditated this week?" Answering this simple question to a partner provides you "Support" to keep going and will be a signal if you are losing focus.

6. Expect resistance from yourself and others; this is natural, but you must be willing to overcome it. A group of good friends is discussing getting together for coffee a couple of times each week at the same time you have decided it is best for you to meditate. It would be easy to say, "Sure, I'll join you," knowing that on those days you would miss meditation. What you should rather say is, "I meditate every morning at that time. Can we start our coffee get-togethers a half hour later?" It may take some negotiations, but you will be surprised that if you look for solutions, you will find them. The key is to be true to your choices and what is right for you.

At the core of these change management guidelines are Skill, Will, and Support. Doing what you planned, therefore, is to make sure you have the skill, will, and support for each of your chosen activities.

Skill

Skill is having the knowledge and experience to do what you want to do. For example, if you want to begin an exercise program for the first time, there are things you need to learn and practice with regards to aerobics, strength, and flexibility training. You need to acquire the skill to ensure you get the most from the activity as well as make sure that you do it in a way that you will not injure yourself.

The good news about building a new skill is that doing so can be fun and it builds your mental energy. To follow our example of starting an exercise program, as you learn how to improve your aerobic capacity, you can enjoy taking brisk walks with friends. All the while, you can be reading and learning from others about how and why aerobic exercise works and how to do it better as you make progress.

One way to assess whether you have the skill you need for an activity is to answer the question, "If I have all of the motivation and support I need, will I have the capability to do what I want to do?" Some have said the question is, "If someone put a gun to my head and said, 'do it,' could I?"

Tom Bloch rose rapidly through the ranks of H&R Block, eventually replacing his father as Chief Executive Officer. In 1995, Tom surprised everybody but himself, when he chose to step down to become an inner city school teacher. His passion for education and his desire to make a difference in the lives of children prompted the significant career change. Tom knew that he needed the training and skills to be the best teacher he could be. He took classes and earned his teaching certificate and began teaching in public schools. After doing so for five years, Tom co-founded the University Academy, a public, inner city charter school in Kansas City. He has also written *Stand for the Best*, a memoir of his journey from CEO to inner city teacher, and he has become an effective advocate for quality education. Tom knew that having a passion for education and teaching is not the same as having the skill to teach.

Our LifeScape, LLC, partner, Bob Miller, retired in 2008. During his career, Bob excelled at and loved coaching others, helping them improve their work performance and manage their careers. Part of his retirement plan was to continue in a coaching capacity by working part-time as an executive and retirement coach. Despite his extensive coaching skills and experience in the corporate environment, he recognized that he did not have all the skills or credentials to meet his retirement goals. Bob engaged with Retirement Options, a company that trains and certifies coaches, and now has his coaching certification. Similarly, Bob is active with Habitat for Humanity and has continued to acquire home-construction skills as he apprentices with experts.

(Alan Spector) When I had the idea to write and publish my first book, I knew that I could form sentences, but had little idea about how to proceed to structure and complete a manuscript, let alone get it published. Before and during the writing of *Baseball: Never Too Old to Play The Game*, I spent as much time learning how to write a book and to publish it as I did actually doing the writing. My local librarian greeted me by first name as I frequented the stacks devouring every book about writing, publishing, and marketing I could find—then I built skills by practicing what I had learned. Although I still have much to learn, I know that I have a foundation on which to build. I needed to build skills first, regardless of the will and support I had to write.

One more way to think about developing skills is how it relates to a hobby. You may have noticed that several personal stories in the book relate to people taking up pottery: Elaine Unell, Trish Martindell, and Joanne Sudman. Each decided to try it and quickly became passionate about the endeavor. They love pottery, in part, because after every session, they know they have been better than in the session before and they have so much to learn in sessions to come. Building skills is an integral part of enjoying the hobby. Perhaps it is not different from writing books or coaching clients or teaching students. Each requires a basic set of skills to get started, and the energy comes from the satisfaction, esteem, challenge, and stimulation gained from continuing to grow the skills.

Will

Will is having the motivation required to do the activity, both now and in the future. It may be more difficult to develop the will for some activities than for others. For example, it might be easy for you to have the motivation to spend more time with your grandchildren, yet more difficult to begin a new exercise program. In either case, you need sufficient will to keep going.

There are many activities in which you may be interested. The question is to which activities are you committed. To measure your level of commitment for something you have included in your plan, ask yourself these two questions, "Am I prepared to take the first step in the next 24 hours?" "Am I prepared to stay focused on the activity for the next 21 days?"

This concept is one of the reasons we placed the worksheets in each chapter of the book. Merely the act of filling them out will help you develop the will to proceed, because the action you took to do so was immediate.

The best change management approaches teach that you are more likely to sustain an activity over time if you begin it immediately after becoming interested and keep going long enough to imbed it in your life. Doing both helps ensure you build your will.

Recall Dr. Richard Gimpelson's story from the "Well-Being"

chapter. Richard had a heart attack and was told by the cardiologist that if he did not change his eating and exercise habits, he would die. Richard immediately began exercising and began and 1800-calorie per day diet, both which he has sustained over time.

When David Nemon, whose model car hobby you read about in "Fun," realized he enjoyed his boyhood passion and tried to convince his ten-year old son to love it as well, David was motivated to get restarted on the hobby himself. He immediately began working on the car kit that he had gotten for his son, and has sustained the fun for more than two decades.

Knowing you would enjoy something (in David Nemon's case) or you must do something (in Richard Gimpelson's case) and actually getting started and keeping it going are two different things. Demonstrate your will to begin each activity by taking the first step and then sustaining it.

Support

Support is having the environment around you to enable your success and having friends and family who encourage your activities. For example, do you have the right food in your home to support healthy nutrition? Do you have access to the right space and equipment to exercise the way you want to or to do your meditation? Do you have work space to build model cars? Do you have access to a library to support the reading you want to do? Is your writing space free from distractions that affect your focus? Regardless of your activity, it is best that your surroundings encourage you.

Support can come from friends and family partnering with you in your activities to help you hold yourself accountable for staying the course. These are the people we referred to earlier as "accountability partners."

Years ago, Jim Hopkins was concerned about his fitness level and concluded that he needed to begin an aerobic exercise routine. He began taking 30 to 45-minute walks with his wife, Jamie, six days per week. Jim and Jamie belong to a couples group that gets together every two months to have a gourmet dinner together, each time choosing a cuisine from a different country. The group has been dining together for almost four decades. Once Jim began walking, he also began to report his progress to the gourmet group, who, every time they got together, asked him how many weeks in a row he had taken his walks. Over the years, Jim has not missed a single week, regardless of weather and of the other things going on in his life, including Chemo treatments for a recent successful bout with cancer. Also over the years, Jim has not neglected to report his progress to his gourmet group, his support group. As of last count, Jim had taken his walks 443 weeks in a row.

Marshall Goldsmith is among the top business consultants in the world. Even though Marshall coaches others, he also has a coach. Marshall has teamed up with a friend. Every day, regardless of where each of them is in the world, they talk to each other. Marshall's friend asks him 17 prearranged questions about things Marshall wants to ensure are going well in his life. Marshall then asks his friend his prearranged questions. The phone call might be sufficient for some, but not for Marshall. He records his answers on a spreadsheet. All of the questions can be answered with "yes," "no," or a number. At the end of the week, he can tell exactly how he is doing. He is holding himself accountable with the help of an accountability partner.

When we decided to collaborate on this book, we spent a great deal of time deciding how to share the effort. One of the things we immediately put in place was a schedule of things we needed to do and assigned one or the other of us to the task. The other thing we did, and continue to do, is schedule Skype sessions or get-togethers to check on whether we were on track with our task assignments. Do we trust each other to deliver our part of the effort? Absolutely! We have worked together for years and are good friends. But, we also know that it is better to be explicit about holding ourselves accountable. We planned a very aggressive schedule for writing and publishing the book and, in large part, because of our mutual support and accountability, held to it.

Some of this accountability followup may seem onerous to you. Certainly there are ways to be more or less rigorous about it and still be successful, and you need to find what works for you. However, the best known approach to making sustainable change is to have an accountability partner. Our suggestion is that you try it and err on the rigorous side until you settle on what works for you. If you are having difficulty establishing new behaviors in your life, take a close look at your support system. You may need to get more rigorous about accountability partners.

There is another aspect of support to consider. It is the support that you can provide to yourself by developing a structure to your day and your life. Many retirees told us they learned that without having a plan and some predictable structure, they found time slipping away. Most took action to add some structure to their lives.

Recall the meditation example at the beginning of this chapter in which the activity was scheduled every day at the same time. You may find some of your activities are best done on a regular schedule instead of trying to fit it in a different time slot from day to day.

You most likely had structure at work. A regular starting time, standard procedures, scheduled meetings, standard reports, and routine phone calls may have been the norm. In retirement, your daily structure is a choice rather than a requirement. If meditation is a 7:00am every-day event, schedule a meeting with yourself and put it on your calendar.

Speaking of calendars, keeping one, along with a task list and a suspense file, will help you support yourself and hold yourself accountable. Again, there are very different ways to approach creating structure for yourself. For example, Keith keeps a running to-do list on a yellow legal pad, crossing off items as he completes them. Alan uses the Outlook Task list, an electronic approach that allows managing tasks through time. Tasks and other reminders can be put away electronically, only to show up on the day you projected you would be interested in seeing them again (this is sometimes known as a "suspense system;" the task item is suspended until a given date).

Regardless of how you proceed to build support for your activities, make sure your environment is right, you have an accountability partner, and you create the life structure that is right for you.

Skill, Will, and Support

As you know by now, we advocate writing things down to help enable making change in your life. We also advocate for simple, useful ways to help do this. Consider using a chart like the one on the next page to guide your thinking about whether you have the skill, will, and support to ensure that you can successfully implement your plan.

You can also use the chart to help you think about and write down your priorities. Simply list the activities from your plan in the order you wish to get them started. When you have filled in your list of activities, complete the skill, will, and support columns.

- In the "Skill" column, put a checkmark (√) if you have the skill or an "x" if you do not. If you do not have the skill, a first step will be to take action to begin to acquire it.
- In the "Will" column, do the same with the checkmark (√) or "x." Recall, knowing if you have the will can be measured by assessing whether you are prepared to take the first step immediately and then sustain it for 21 days. If you feel you do not have the will, devise a first step you can take quickly and an approach to stay with the activity.
- In the "Support" column, write the name of the person who is your accountability partner for that activity. If you have already recruited your partner, put a checkmark (√) by the name; if not, just have the name until your recruiting is complete. If you do not have anyone identified, place an "x." You may decide that there are some activities for which you do not believe you need a partner. For those, simply put a checkmark (√). If this does not work out, you can add a partner later.
- Your objective, to maximize your probability of success, is to have checkmarks in all of the columns for each of your activities.

If you need to, you can use the chart repeated on the worksheet in this chapter, use extra paper, or create a chart on your computer.

Activities	Skill	Will	Support

Visit www.YourRetirementQuest.com to find the necessary forms to use. This is where you can combine the Start/Stop/Continue activities you have chosen for your plan with the "Support Partner" you have chosen for each activity. Filling it out will help round out your thinking about your initial plan.

Practice Retirement

Mahatma Gandhi said, "An ounce of practice is worth more than a ton of preaching." For those who are still anticipating retirement, you have the opportunity to practice it—to begin early to do what you have planned. If you are already retired, the principle is to act now.

Secret 8: Action
- Retirement begins now; you never know what tomorrow may bring.
- Don't wait to act on what is important to you—act now, even if you have yet to retire –"practice retirement."

We have had attendees at our LifeScape, LLC seminars ask us if we would share our model with youth groups and young adults. These attendees recognized that the key elements of a fulfilling retirement are also the key elements of a fulfilling life, regardless what phase you are in. Therefore, if you are still working in your primary career and in the anticipation stage of retirement, questions you might want to ask yourself are, "Why wait for retirement to build my life around the key elements?" "What can I be doing now that will get me started on my retirement plan?"

If you are still working, it would be in your best interest to begin practicing retirement, which would also be in the best interest of your employer.

There is a disturbing business trend; employees of all ages are becoming less engaged in their work. As a result, morale, productivity, and business results suffer. For the most experienced generation of employees, those 55 to 64, disengagement may result from being distracted by an uncertainty about their future, both while still at work and into retirement.

The demographics of this segment of the workforce is interesting in that it is the fastest growing and many are delaying retirement for financial and health insurance reasons. Yet, at the same time, about 10,000 baby boomers are retiring each day in the U.S. The opportunity for both companies and their experienced employees is to bring more certainty to each employee's future. Doing so will help the employee reengage and be more productive at work, while also setting a course for a more fulfilling retirement.

Envision an employee, you for instance, who has both a financial and, importantly, a nonfinancial plan for your future. You have also begun to get experience with some of the things you plan doing in retirement. You are more certain about your future because you can see what it will look like and have a plan to make it successful. You are more engaged and productive at work.

The productivity gain satisfies the employer's concern about you practicing retirement. What is in it for you, the future retiree? There are several things to your benefit. You will be field testing your plan, and if you find activities that do not work out, you can rethink your plan before you retire. Some people have a difficult time transitioning from full work to full retirement. When you practice retirement, you ease into that transition. Finally, and perhaps most importantly, you will be doing the things earlier that you decided would make your life more fulfilling.

Practicing retirement does not mean you stop coming to work. It means you find ways to get experience with your retirement plans earlier. If you plan to spend more time cooking when you retire, take a cooking class one evening a week. If you plan to read the classics, start one and set aside some time each week for it. If you plan to compete in bridge tournaments, add one or two bridge evenings per month to your schedule. If you look forward to travelling more, take some day trips or long weekends.

Practicing retirement is good for you and good for your employer.

If you are already retired, Secret #8 applies to you as well. You are reading this book because you are looking forward to a more meaningful retirement. To achieve it, you will need to make some changes. Act now.

Key Learning about "Doing What You Planned"

1. Doing your plan is as important as developing your plan. The results for those setting New Year's resolutions tell the change story. On average, a person makes the same resolution ten times before acting on it. Fifty percent of people break their promise to themselves in a very short time. Less than 10% make real sustainable change.

2. The flip side is that the benefits derived from making sustainable change in your life are worth the effort. Envision living the retirement you have dreamed of.

3. The proven way to successfully adopt new habits is to consciously ensure you have the skill, will, and support you need. This includes the critical step of ensuring you have an accountability partner to support you.

4. Retirement is a learning journey; you can try activities that intrigue you and not worry about them not working out perfectly. These activities teach you more about what is important to you.

Getting Started

1. Start small and strive to get a "quick win." Do not try to change too many aspects of your life at once. Choose a new habit or activity to focus on for 21 days, start it now, and imbed it in your life. Recruit a partner to help you succeed.

2. Develop an approach to manage your time by bringing structure to your life in a way that works for you.

3. Think about one or more times you were successful bringing change into your life. What worked for you then? Reapply those approaches to changes in your retirement plan.

4. Put notes with simple reminders about your behavior change in visible places, for example, on your refrigerator, bathroom mirror, or desk.

5. Schedule some time with yourself each week to quickly assess how you are doing. When you have established a new behavior

or activity, take the time to recognize your success.

6. If you have yet to retire, find ways to practice your planned retirement activities to become more certain about your plan and to be more energized and productive while you are still working.

"Doing What You Planned" Worksheet

Personal Assessment: Rate the following statement from 1 to 5:
1 = This statement is far from describing my plan implementation.
5 = This statement fully describes my plan implementation.

"I know it takes skill, will, and support to make change in my life and I am applying this to my retirement plans."

Rating: 1   2   3   4   5

Activities	Skill	Will	Support

Personal thoughts about how to ensure I do what I planned:

_____

_____

_____

_____

_____

_____

Chapter 19

Renewing Your Plan

"One thing life taught me—if you are interested, you never have to look for new interests. They come to you."
Eleanor Roosevelt

"The doors we open and close each day decide the lives we live."
Flora Whittemore

Do You Know?

Seventy-five percent of families will be involved with elder care, having a significant impact on their time, energy, and resources.

Sixty percent of college graduates return home after graduation.

Forty-four percent of Americans ages 45 to 55 have both living parents and children under 21.

Ten percent of all Americans with grandchildren under the age of five are providing extensive care-giving for those children.

Over 40% of people ages 50 to 64 report difficulty with at least one daily physical function and many report difficulty with more than one function.

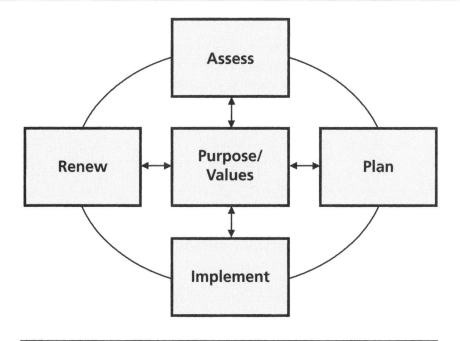

What is "Renewing Your Plan?"

You now have a retirement plan and a strategy to implement it. These will get you off to a great start. However, life circumstances change, sometimes in positive ways, sometimes negatively. When change occurs, it may be time to alter your plan. That is why one of the blocks in the planning model is "Renew"—to keep your plan fresh.

Fr. Raymond J. de Souza is the priest of Sacred Heart of Mary Parish on Wolfe Island, Ontario, Canada; the Roman Catholic chaplain of Queen's University, teaching in the Department of Economics at the University; and a columnist for the *National Post* newspaper. Fr. de Souza provided an insightful perspective about life and how to think about ongoing renewal when he wrote:

> *"For a long time it had seemed to me that life was*
> *about to begin – real life.*
> *But there was always some obstacle in the way,*
> *something to be gotten through first,*
> *Some unfinished business, time still to be served, or*
> *a debt to be paid.*
> *Then life would begin.*
> *At last it dawned on me that these obstacles were*
> *my life.*
> *This perspective has helped me to see there is no*
> *way to happiness.*
> *Happiness is the way. So treasure every moment*
> *you have."*

Recall the John Bolton quotation, "A plan is only something from which to deviate." Bolton was teaching that a plan needs to be current. He was also teaching us to assume that any plan would change and, therefore, to periodically reassess it to take into account new circumstances and opportunities. With Bolton's guidance in mind, there are four things to do to keep your plan fresh. In the following sections of the chapter, we will look at each of these in more detail:

1. Recognize when life circumstances change sufficiently to warrant renewal of your plan.

2. Seek and be open to opportunities that will enable you to enhance your plan.

3. Be sensitive to the possibility that you can enter retirement's Disenchantment stage, and if you do, rejuvenate your plan to get back on track.

4. Even if circumstances or opportunities have not substantially changed for some time, periodically check your plan to make sure it is still right.

Secret 9: Resiliency
- Retirement life is always evolving, sometimes in positive ways, sometimes not.
- Be resilient—be open to new opportunities, be receptive to change, and accept the reality of and adapt to setbacks.

True Resiliency

Resiliency is a critical component of being willing and able to renew your plan as you age. It is the ability to adapt to changing life circumstances and to be open to new opportunities.

Kathy Ison is neither retired nor within a decade of being so, but her work and family experiences have taught her the importance of having the resiliency to adapt to changes in life circumstances. She also has a powerful perspective about retirement because of the work she does.

For 32 years, Kathy has been working with the elderly, first as a Physical Therapist for Medicare patients going through rehabilitation and, more recently, as the Vice-President of Affordable Housing and In-Home Services for the Episcopal Retirement Homes. In her early career, she worked closely with a nun who believed in treating people holistically, helping patients heal by addressing both their physical and spiritual needs. Kathy saw firsthand numerous examples of patients getting better with the help of meditation, visualization, deep breathing techniques, prayer, and the support of others. She personally observed patients developing energy in all of its dimensions—physical, emotional, mental, and purpose. She also observed the importance of resiliency as the seniors adapted to their new life circumstances, despite their age.

Kathy Ison

Kathy was then challenged to show her own resiliency and sustain her own energy. Four years ago, her husband died unexpectedly, and she became a single parent, rearing four sons. With the support of family and friends and with a willingness to accept help, Kathy has developed a balance of work and family. She exhibits all of the traits of a resilient person. Along with her openness to seeking and accepting help, she is in touch with her own feelings, makes tough and realistic priority choices, and looks for the positive meaning of the changes in her life circumstances. In that regard, Kathy recognized when it was right for her to change roles at work to spend more time at home. She chose to focus on what is most important in life, her sons, instead of worrying about less important things, like how neat the house was. In addition, she worked with her sons to take on new responsibilities around the house, helping them personally grow despite the loss of their father. Not only is Kathy resilient and renewing her plan, but she is teaching her sons to do the same.

Kathy has built resiliency into her life and her character by learning to both take advantage of opportunities (e.g., learning from the nun) and adapt to changes in life circumstances (i.e., the unexpected death of her husband and the rearing of four sons as a single parent). She renews her life plan frequently, and when ready for retirement, she will be well-positioned for a smooth transition.

Our Gypsy Souls

Marc Golubock is retired from a long career with the Federal Department of Justice. He lives in Phoenix, although he and his wife, Susan, spend a month each summer in New England or other cooler summer spots and as much time as they can in France, where they lived for several years during Marc's career. Marc does some consulting, loves good food and good wine, and is an avid tennis player. A decade ago, Marc began to feel pain in one of his hips while playing tennis and soon found it persisting. Shortly thereafter, the pain, caused by arthritis, became debilitating; affecting not only his tennis, but his whole life. Marc tried to resolve the problem through medication, exercise, and everything else he thought might help, yet there was no relief. He decided on hip replacement surgery. Five years later, the same progression occurred in his other hip—again, surgery. Did the chain of events over the time period affect Marc's life plans? Yes, they did, but he confronted his new circumstances, adjusted his life to account for them, and moved on. Oh, and Marc is still an avid tennis player, albeit doubles instead of singles. Marc has two new hips and a renewed plan.

Marc Golubock

(Alan Spector) Ann and I moved to Cincinnati in 1976 to work in Procter & Gamble's headquarters city. Just before Ann retired in 2001, our first grandson, Jordan, was born in St. Louis, where Ann and I both grew up. We decided that even though we lived 360 miles away, we would ensure that Jordan knew us well as he grew up; we would visit St. Louis every month as part of our retirement plan. We continued to visit frequently after Jordan's brother, Aaron, was born. In 2008, our third grandson, Jake, was born in Boston, and we added frequent trips there as well. Jake now has a baby sister, Zoe. Grandchildren visits and all of the other travel we were doing meant we were seldom in Cincinnati, causing our ties there to weaken. In 2009, we decided to move to St. Louis and travel frequently to Boston. The blessing of grandchildren changed our plan.

Ann Chisko is retired from a career as a Mathematics Professor and one-time Head of the Math Department at Raymond Walters College, a branch of the University of Cincinnati. While Ann was still working, her once-vibrant parents, who lived 750 miles away, were beginning to experience the effects of aging. Ann traveled frequently to make sure they were doing well in their independent living situation, but concluded they required more care than she could provide long distance. She moved them into an assisted living facility near her. Although her parents were now nearby, she was spending much of her time and emotional energy responding to their needs. She had intended to continue to chair the Math Department, but decided not to do so because of the support she was providing her parents. Without the income from heading the department, Ann's financial plans were affected, but emotionally, it was the right choice. Her father passed away first, then her mother some years later. Whether Ann was traveling to help them, supporting them nearby, or dealing with their deaths, the circumstances changed her plans.

Ann Chisko and John Balling

Just before Ann retired, she reconnected with a former friend, John Balling, who lived in Webster, New York, and they began a long distance relationship. John, who plays piano professionally, began taking some time off and eventually spent a third of his time with Ann in Cincinnati. After Ann's mother passed away, John and Ann decided that they enjoyed splitting their time between Cincinnati and Webster, so they continued to do so. As Ann says, "It appeals to our gypsy souls." Like Ann, John's life circumstances changed. He renewed his plan as had Ann, and they moved on—together.

A variety of circumstances caused Kathy, Marc, Ann, John, and the Spectors to change their plans. The common theme through their stories, however, is that each recognized the need to change, accepted a new reality, took responsibility, adjusted plans, and moved on.

The human condition is such that, as you grow older, you can expect to be confronted by more issues with less time between them. They may be the illness or death of a spouse or other close relative, your own health issues, or decreased mobility. Having a plan and being experienced at renewing it will become more important as you age.

The objective, therefore, is to get into the planning cycle to address new opportunities and new challenges. The recipe is to assess your situation, establish your plan, implement it, renew it—then reassess your situation and repeat. You will gain skill and confidence at deciding which circumstances warrant a plan change and which do not as you continue through the planning cycle. This is what renewal of your plan is all about.

Actively Listening

There is a very long list of personally fulfilling activities from which to choose. However, when you created your initial plan in the earlier chapters, your list of possibilities was limited to those you personally knew about, ideas from friends and family with whom you consulted, and ideas that inspired you from the stories of others in this book.

Your possibilities list may have been sufficient to get you started; but, as you play out your plan, it is likely you will be looking to expand your horizons of opportunity. Also, because the key element "Growth" is now an integral part of your holistic plan, you will be on the prowl for new and challenging variety.

How will you seek and find new opportunities to consider as you renew your plan? Importantly, how will you respond to opportunities that come out of the blue to present themselves? One measure of the success of your plan will be whether or not you are constantly coming across new opportunities. If you are, you are likely living fully, because your attitude is positive, your energy level is high, you are well-connected, pursuing your passions, growing, having fun, and valuing your plan.

Opportunities are all around you. The best way to find them is to actively listen and look for them, be sensitive to their presence, and accept them as being right for you—said another way, being open to the possibilities.

When you are or were working, you may have even tended to block out much of what was going on outside of your career. You were busy with career and family and the few outside interests that you loved to do. Other opportunities may have shown up to you as distractions, and you got into the habit of selectively ignoring them. To change that habit to become an active listener, you may need to force yourself to start out by being hyper-aware.

You might learn about a fundraiser at your church intended to help children in need in your area. You care deeply for children and are looking for meaningful ways to give back to your community. If you are actively listening for opportunities, this will show up as one you want to pursue—volunteering to help with the fundraiser. Not only will you be pursuing passions and giving back, but you will also be more connected with your church community, and more opportunities will likely show up in the future.

A friend might mention to you that he has been asked to make a motivational speech to an organization, but he knows nothing about developing a visual presentation that he wants to accompany his talk. If you are actively listening for opportunities, you will hear this as more than just information from a friend. Rather, if you have the skill he needs, you might offer to help him. Doing so increases connectedness, allows you to participate in his effort of giving back, and gets you involved in what could open up more opportunities for you in the future.

You might read in the newspaper that your local university is starting a lifelong learning program for people over 50. You have been looking for ways to keep your mind active, have wanted to learn more about photography to improve your burgeoning interest, and see that a photography class is being offered during the program's first session. If you had not been actively seeking new challenges and interests, this might have been just another column in the newspaper. But you jump at the chance to get involved, and it turns into an activity that provides you with personal growth and connectedness to new classmates, enhances your pursuit of a new passion, and becomes just plain fun.

Each of these opportunities could have passed you by unnoticed had you not been actively listening and looking for them. You could have said to your church, "I really hope the fundraiser goes well, and I'll donate a few dollars."

You could have said to your friend, "I wish you luck with your motivational speech."

You could have read the lifelong learning article and said to yourself, "Gee, that's interesting; someday I might look into that."

But what you said to yourself was, "I've been looking for opportunities just like this; I'm going to act—now."

You will find that some of the opportunities you choose to take advantage of will not work out. That is great, because you will have learned more about yourself, your plan, and what your fulfilling retirement should look like. If you never fail, it is an indication that you are not stretching yourself sufficiently to help you grow. Just as weightlifting builds muscles by breaking them down so that when they grow back, they are stronger, so will you be stronger after failures because of what you have learned.

This is where attitude comes back into the picture. In *Retire Right*, Frederick Fraunfelder, MD and James Gilbaugh, MD propose that because optimistic people believe they will succeed, it makes sense that they tend to take more risks. These same people are open to opportunities and life's possibilities, an important component of successful aging and retirement.

Here is another recipe: be optimistic, actively listen and look, act on the opportunities that show up, fail occasionally, learn from the failures, build on successes, and repeat.

Superman

(Alan Spector) I gained a perspective about how to respond to opportunities while I was still working. One of my brilliant colleagues was Ron Visscher, PhD. Ron had a wonderful ability to balance his expansive and, sometimes, "out there" thinking with his practical side. One afternoon some 30 years ago, the practical side lost out. I was walking back to my office, which was only a couple of doors from Ron's. I came around the corner and saw Ron by himself in the hallway, staring at the ceiling. I stopped and watched him for awhile. Ron kept staring and then suddenly thrust his arms toward the ceiling. After watching him do this again a few moments later, I could not stand it any longer.

"Ron, what are you doing? Are you OK?"

"Al, do you know what would be worse than not being Superman?" Ron asked, still staring at the white, perforated, soundproofing panels of the hallway ceiling.

"No, Ron, I hadn't thought about it."

"Well I have—being Superman and not knowing it." Once more he thrust his arms toward the ceiling.

I started to say something, although I cannot recall how I could have possibly responded to that.

"Al," he went on, speaking seriously, "someday, you might come down this hallway, and there will be a hole in the ceiling, papers strewn everywhere from the gust of wind, and I will be gone."

He walked into his office and did not look back.

Was Ron Visscher out of his mind? No, but I must admit to being more than a little concerned about him at the time. On the drive home, I reflected on my Ron Visscher/Clark Kent experience. I concluded that Ron and I had a very profound discussion, although I was too shortsighted to recognize it immediately. What I believe Ron was really thinking about was whether he was living up to his own potential. What if he were Superman but did not know it? What if he had more capability than he was using, but did not know it?

The next day, as soon as I knew Ron was in his office, I stopped by to ask him if I understood our conversation correctly. He merely smiled. I must admit, every now and then, I would come around that corner and check the ceiling, expecting to see at least a dent.

Ron Visscher

I will never forget that discussion. Nor will I forget the lesson Ron taught me. Am I living up to my potential? Am I searching for and acting on opportunities that are available to me? Am I giving myself the chances to be more than I am and more than I thought I could be?

I thought about Ron's lesson throughout my career. I was fortunate during those 33 years to have opportunities frequently come my way, helping me test and grow my capabilities. That was the nature of the company and our business. However, when I retired, opportunities were not fed to me. I learned I needed to find them on my own.

Three decades later, Ron Visscher is making a difference in my retirement plan and, therefore, my life. Maybe he is Superman.

Rejuvenation and Periodic Reviews

We have discussed renewing your plan to accommodate changing life circumstances and to take advantage of new opportunities. The third reason to reassess and renew your plan is when you recognize you have entered or are even approaching the Disenchantment stage of retirement.

In her book, *The How of Happiness*, Sonja Lyubomirsky

describes "hedonic adaptation," sometimes referred to as the "hedonic treadmill." The concept is that our level of happiness tends to be moderated, because we adapt to new conditions and make them part of our new normal. An example in the workplace would be the effect of getting a raise. You are thrilled to receive it, but the elation does not last long as you incorporate the additional money into your current lifestyle.

In retirement, hedonic adaptation has a similar effect. Perhaps you have found an organization for which to volunteer. You are energized by the opportunity and immediately see the benefit to those you are helping. You are spending two mornings each week doing this great work. However, while the work remains important and you are still feeling as though you are contributing, the weekly sessions become part of your routine. When this goes on for awhile and mixes with several other activities feeling the same way, you may begin to feel bored, somewhat in a rut.

We are not proposing that you should stop doing this work. Rather, we contend that such feelings could be the onset of entering the Disenchantment stage, and it is, therefore, worthwhile to trigger a renewal of your plan. In this way, instead of blindly going forward, you will be making overt choices about what you want to Start, Stop, and Continue.

It is also likely that you will go through some time periods in which life circumstances have not substantially changed and you have not become disenchanted. This probably means that you are living a fulfilling retirement and all is well.

That being said, experience shows that doing a review of your plan every three months is about the right period of time. Three months is long enough to make sure you are not spending all of your time planning, yet short enough such that if your plan is beginning to grow stale, you can renew it before too long. One way to ensure that you are disciplined about reassessing your plan is to schedule periodic renewals, putting them on your calendar.

Another reason for reassessing your plan periodically is to validate for yourself that you are a competent planner. If you have a plan that is working for you, you may choose to simply continue what you are doing in all of its aspects. When you do that, you can say to yourself, "I am planning well. When I change my plan the next time for whatever reason, I will be confident in what I choose to do differently."

However, if you find you are simply continuing the same plan for many three-month periods in a row, it may be an indication that you are not stretching yourself sufficiently to grow and not staying sharp and fulfilled. Balancing between continuing the plan when it is working and not going too long between changes is part of the renewal process.

During these periodic reviews, you can assess how you are doing and whether your plan needs renewal by making the following candid observations about yourself. You can also ask a support partner to be available to give you his or her perspective about how you are doing.

It is likely not necessary to make many changes if time if flying by, you have plenty of energy, you look forward to starting your day, and your investments of time and money are aligned with your purpose and values.

It is likely time to refresh your plan if you observe that on many days, you are irritable, you are frequently ill, you are doing the same thing every day, or you are always thinking and talking about the "good old days." Think about other observations that would be indicators for you to let you know renewal is in order.

When you renew your plan for any reason, it is a perfect time to also revisit your life purpose and core values as well as the right time to ensure they are consistent with your renewed plan.

Regardless of what causes you to renew your plan, you will find it energizing and satisfying to do so. Once more, "A plan is only something from which to deviate."

Key Learning about "Renewing Your Plan"

1. Renewal is a natural aspect of life and essential as you age.
2. The times to renew your plan are when life circumstances change in a meaningful way, either positively or negatively, when new opportunities come your way, when you are approaching or are in Disenchantment, and when you periodically review your plan and find it beginning to grow stale.
3. Renewal begins with an open, candid assessment of your current reality and a revitalization of your dreams and your plans to achieve them.

Getting Started

1. Set up a schedule on your calendar (suggested to be quarterly) to do a candid personal assessment to determine if the time is right to renew your plan.

2. Use one or more of these techniques to periodically prompt your thinking about renewal.

    a. Use the reasons for renewal on pages 234 and 235 to determine if your plan needs to be refreshed.

    b. Revisit the assessment statements and ratings from your key element worksheets to determine if you are on track toward your fulfilling retirement.

    c. Look at your calendar and checkbook. Are your investments of time and money consistent with your purpose and values? If not, it may be time for renewal.

3. When you do your periodic assessment, ask a close friend to give you his or her point of view. Also, and perhaps most importantly, be open to your own feelings, which will be signaling to you if you need to change.

4. Periodically scan your local newspaper and relevant web sites, which frequently have lists and details of volunteer opportunities, cultural events, and other activities that may open up new horizons for you or may be complementary to other things you are already doing.

5. If you conclude you need to renew your plan, revisit your life purpose and your core values. Are they still right for you? Are you living them? What changes do you need to make in your plan to realign yourself with your purpose and values?

6. As you renew your plan, take all of the key elements into account and rewrite your Start/Stop/Continue actions.

"Renewing Your Plan" Planning Worksheet

Personal Assessment: Rate the following statement from 1 to 5:
1 = This statement is far from describing my renewal plans.
5 = This statement fully describes my renewal plans.

"I am confident I will keep my retirement plan fresh by renewing it as life circumstances change and opportunities present themselves."

Rating: 1   2   3   4   5

My next quarterly plan review will be on: _____ (fill in date)

Thoughts about "Renewing My Plan":

_____

_____

_____

_____

_____

_____

_____

_____

_____

_____

The one person in my life who can best help me to implement my immediate next step regarding Renewing My Plan is

_____

Chapter 20

Living Fully

"To finish the moment,
to find the journey's end in every step of the road,
to live the greatest number of good hours is wisdom."
Ralph Waldo Emerson

"Lost time is never found again."
Benjamin Franklin

What is "Living Fully?"

The retiree's wife asks, "What are you going to do today?"

"Nothing," he replies.

"Isn't that what you did yesterday?"

"I wasn't finished."

While an occasional recovery day of "doing nothing" is called for, too many such days is the opposite of "living fully."

Living fully is enjoying a holistic, balanced life. It is balancing activity and relaxation; time for others and time for self; attention to mind, body, and spirit; and living across all of the key elements. Living fully is jumping out of bed in the morning to get started for the day. Living fully is learning and engaging and growing and playing and stretching yourself. Living fully is being interested and interesting, being curious, being a good friend, a great brother, and better grandmother. Living fully is *knowing* you are living fully.

You have developed your plan and know how to implement and renew it. It is time to get started on your journey, to leave the book, but to know that it is nearby for future reference. This chapter, therefore, will not have a learning summary, or suggestions on getting started, or a worksheet. Our intent here is to leave you with some additional perspective about living fully and living a fulfilling life as you go on to live yours.

Secret 10: Time
- Time is the most precious resource you have—you can never get it back
- Apply the LifeScape Solutions™ approach to make the best use of your time in the best years of your life.

Splendid Torch

The Irish playwright, George Bernard Shaw, lived fully to age 94. His body of work was extensive (e.g., *Pygmalion*, *The Devil's*

Disciple), and he is the only person in history to win both the Nobel Prize for Literature and an Oscar. He was known for his combination of intellect and wit. It was Shaw who said, "My way of joking is to tell the truth. It's the funniest joke in the world."

Shaw wrote the following poem, one that could be considered the anthem for the retiree who is living fully.

This is the true joy of life.
The being used for a purpose
Recognized by yourself as a mighty one.
The being a force of nature
Instead of a feverish, selfish
Little clod of ailments and grievances
Complaining that the world will not
Devote itself to making you happy.
I am of the opinion that my life
Belongs to the whole community
And as long as I live,
It is my privilege to do for it
Whatever I can.
I want to be thoroughly
Used up when I die,
For the harder I work the more I live.
I rejoice in life for its own sake.
Life is no brief candle to me.
It is a sort of splendid torch
Which I've got hold of
For the moment
And I want to make it burn

"Everything I do is fun."

Natalie Kauffman recently read a newspaper article about a local radio station that was planning to air racially and ethnically charged commercials supporting a candidate from a local white supremacist organization. She sprang into action, and within days, was engaged in conversations with the Anti-Defamation League, her Representative's and Senator's offices in Washington, and the FCC.

She also established an ongoing dialogue with the radio station's manager, who began working with Natalie to find a way to legally not run the commercials. Natalie Kaufmann is 76 years old, all of four-foot nine-inches tall, fiery, and somewhat cynical (in fact, she says, "I have an undergraduate degree in skepticism and a graduate degree in cynicism).

Natalie is young at heart, has a quick self-deprecating sense of humor that she believes is part of what gets her through life's trials and tribulations, has been retired since 2005, and is passionate about life.

Natalie Kauffman

Natalie views herself as actually being twice retired, once at age 58 and again at age 71. After earning her business degree from Webster University at age 42, she worked for several companies in marketing and sales. She never really felt this work was meaningful and retired from full-time work to pursue a substitute teaching career, where she primarily taught languages, German, Spanish, and French, at the high school level.

Her passion for languages did not end when she retired from teaching. Natalie is a lifelong learner and has continued to take classes at a local university, including multiple courses on Greek mythology and Russian literature. Her learning extends beyond the university; she is also a member of OASIS, a program in many cities around the country, whose mission is to "enrich the lives of mature adults by engaging them in lifelong learning..." Natalie is also an active member of the Round Table, an adjunct of OASIS that discusses current events and other topics of common interest.

Her greatest passion, however, is the St. Louis Jewish Film Festival, where she has been volunteering and chairing committees for the 14 years since its inception. Natalie dedicates virtually fulltime hours to make the festival successful throughout the year. She has also initiated the St. Louis Film Society, which screens more provocative films and conducts panel discussion after each film. These film organizations enable Natalie to pursue a passion and give back to and be connected with her community, as well as provide her with ever-important self-esteem.

Natalie's life is full of learning, volunteering, advocating for political causes, attending to her well-being by working out for an hour every morning, and spending time with her family, including her son, Brad, and daughter-in-law, Liz. She also loves cultural events and attends as often as possible with her husband, Al, who, in his early-80s, still works fulltime.

Natalie's retirement is a mix of doing those things that are always her top priorities and being spontaneous at the same time to take advantage of ad hoc opportunities that come her way. She views herself as a "rabble-rouser" and believes her curiosity, persistence, engagement, and commitment to lifelong learning keep her young. When asked what she does just for fun, Natalie responded without hesitation, "Everything I do is fun, or I wouldn't be doing it."

The Gift of Retirement

When Harry Kangis had the opportunity to retire at age 51 after a 20-year corporate career, he recalled a retiring friend's comment from a few years earlier, "All my life, I've had either time and no money or money and no time. Now I have the gift of both financial security and time, and I owe it to myself to use this gift wisely."

To use his gift wisely, Harry developed a plan based on an assessment of the amount of time he would have the opportunity to fill to replace his previous work time. He intuitively knew that he wanted a diversity of activities that would lead to a balanced, meaningful life. To replace his five "work days," Harry created five hypothetical "retirement days":

- **One day for living life at a more sensible pace**—e.g., reading the newspaper, catching up with friends
- **One day taking better care of himself**—e.g., exercising, more sleep, less stress
- **One day for giving back**—e.g., volunteering even more than he had in the past
- **One day for traveling** with his wife, Julia, and enjoying his children and grandchildren
- **One day for paid work**—creating a business about which he was passionate

The key to making it all work was identifying and developing a business that was challenging, rewarding, and compelling without being all-consuming, so that he did not squander his new gift of retirement.

Harry began preparing for and practicing retirement several years early. He spent time outside of work investigating where there might be an unmet client need that he could help meet based on his experience and skills. He studied how to startup and build a consulting business, and actually "test marketing" himself with potential clients. Importantly, Harry had taken advantage of opportunities to volunteer with non-profits, like the Nature Conservancy, to help them with their strategy development. This gave him the personal satisfaction of helping those who were doing important work, and it created personal connections that would be beneficial to him once he retired.

As a result of his preretirement preparation and practice, when Harry retired, he was able to quickly transition to his new life phase— beginning his first paid client engagement in month one. Harry built on his career experience and his pro-bono non-profit work to develop a consulting business that helps companies develop an effective strategic plan. He also collaborated with some valued friends on two other businesses they started. The collaboration provided Harry with personal contact and professional collaboration, contributing to both his personal growth and his connectedness.

While Harry is passionate about helping his client companies and their employees, he also remains true to his retirement plan, balancing work with family, friends, giving back, and well-being. Harry assures the balance by constantly asking himself what he wants his business to be (e.g., how much travel, where to do his work, who to work with) and what he wants it not to be (e.g., what not to repeat that drove him "nuts" during his corporate career).

As a result of his introspection and planning, Harry has been able to create a retirement business even more successful than imagined, while also spending the time he envisioned with his grandchildren and traveling the world and, thus far, visiting 51 of the 57 U. S. National Parks with Julia. The love of time with his family is evidenced by the photo he posted on his business web site—not the typical business head shot of Harry alone, but one with Julia and their five grandchildren.

Harry and Julia Kangis with their five grandchildren

Harry continues to make time to be an active grandfather, relax, stay healthy, see the world, and give back, while being as busy as he wants to be with his paid consulting. Harry did his homework early, prepared for and practiced his retirement plan, and now lives by it. He is active, busy, curious, connected, and making a real difference in the world—living the gift of retirement.

Living Fully is Winning Out

Icy Williams retired in September 2009, and cannot imagine how she had any time to work, even though toward the end of her 29-year career, she was still working long hours. Her husband, Clarence, tells her, "I thought you were going to slow down a bit."

Although she is busy, balance is the key to Icy's early retirement years. She spreads her time across a number of activities, assuring that she has plenty of time for her family, her church, her hobbies, and her passions.

Icy Williams

When she retired, Icy was the leader of her company's program to ensure that minority and women-owned companies were an integral part of the supply chain. This was more than a job for her. She fundamentally believed that she could make a difference in the African-American community by helping minority businesses have an opportunity to develop and compete. When she retired, she immediately began to focus a significant portion of her retirement time on continuing to act on her belief.

Icy volunteers as a consultant to the Diverse Manufacturing Supply Chain Alliance, a national organization that provides support for businesses that share a commitment to the creation and retention of jobs at minority manufacturers in minority communities. Icy also volunteers as the Chair for the National Sustainability Coalition, a non-profit organization that brings professionals together from multiple disciplines to foster environmental awareness and capability among small and diverse businesses in America.

She also volunteers at her church, leading the "Women's Conference." The conference energizes and enables women across generations in the surrounding neighborhoods to make a difference in their communities.

When we contacted Icy to interview her for the book, she was not immediately available, because she and Clarence had taken their two grandchildren for a five-day long weekend to a local indoor water park. Icy was in the delivery room when her eight-year old granddaughter was born and feels a special connection. She is likewise attached to her "extremely active" two-year old grandson. She and Clarence enjoy their time with the grandchildren and are lobbying to take them, without the parents, on a six-week trip.

The trip would be to the Williams' second home near their family outside of Houston. Spending time there allows them to visit with family and get some quiet time on their own. Icy is an avid reader of murder mysteries and an occasional history book, a lifelong lover of fishing, which she uses as her time for full relaxation and personal reflection, and a dedicated walker, which she uses to stay in shape. The Texas home, which is on the water, allows her the time and environment to delve into all three hobbies. Having the grandchildren there would be a wonderful bonus.

Icy and Clarence spend as much time together as possible in each locale. Clarence, a former Green Bay Packer defensive end, manages a travel agency that gives him some time flexibility. He is deeply involved with the Masons, their church, and following his favorite sports teams. Clarence annually returns to Green Bay to enjoy the Packer alumni weekend, which frequently involves a golf tournament.

Icy's biggest problem in retirement is that she has not learned how to say, "No." She is constantly contacted for advice and asked to participate in one thing or another. So far, she has been able to maintain her balance, but is on guard to make sure that living fully does not turn into living overloaded. Living fully is winning out.

Enjoy the Rewards

Natalie, Harry, and Icy are living fully. Each of their retirement lives is unique as are those of the others you have read about in the book—just as your retirement life will be unique to you. You have a plan that has taken who you are and your particular life circumstances into account. You know how to implement that plan, and you know when and how to renew it as your life circumstances change.

You have every right to believe that the retirement you have envisioned for yourself is possible. You have embraced your future, because you have brought certainty to it. It is now time to enjoy that future.

Early in the book, we acknowledged that, for any number of reasons, you may be entering or in retirement with a healthy dose of anxiety. We asked you to suspend that feeling through the course of the book, predicting that when you finished learning more about what is possible and planning for your future, you would feel that anxiety reduced. We hope that is the case for you now.

We also hope that you enjoyed learning from others and are well-prepared to take full advantage of the *10 Secrets for Creating and Living a Fulfilling Retirement*. May you enjoy the rewards of *Your Retirement Quest*.

Appendix

How to Use This Book

We hope the book serves you in two ways. First, it provides you with the insights to envision a fulfilling retirement and a practical approach to planning for it. Second, it can be a ready-reference while you are going through it the first time and throughout your retirement years. Because it is a reference book, we suggest the following:

1. Write in the book as you go—use the worksheets and the margins. You can return to your personal notes while reading the book and in the future.
2. Navigate www.YourRetirementQuest.com to revisit key concepts and complete forms and keep in a place that works best for you. Whether you write in the book, create your own forms, and/or use the forms on the web site, you will be creating and capturing your initial plan and be able to revise it over time.

You will find each chapter structured to provide you with information and insights about its subject matter and worksheets to help you develop your unique personal retirement plan. All but Chapters 1 and 20 include:

*   A "Do You Know" section to whet your appetite to learn about each subject area.
*   A "What is..." section to introduce the subject matter by providing you more detailed information.

- Real-life stories of people who have relevant experiences and learning. When one of these stories is about one of us, we have begun it with our name in parentheses and written it in first person.
- A brief chapter summary of "Key Learning about..."
- A list of "Getting Started" suggestions for you to consider as you begin your planning. We chose, in general, not to provide you with specific examples of activities, because that would be too prescriptive. Rather, our intent is to help you begin your own adventure of discovery, from which you can derive the activities that are right for your unique life circumstances.
- The final component is a worksheet to help you capture your thoughts about the chapter's subject and ideas about what you may want to include in your plan.

When you see this icon in the book, it will introduce one of the *10 Secrets for Creating and Living a Fulfilling Retirement.* The secrets will be introduced nearest the information that directly explains them in more detail.

The book is intended to be read and used in the order presented, but you will also find it easy to revisit subject matter to assist you in creating your retirement plan. By the book's end, you will have created your personal plan, know how to make it happen, and be prepared to renew your plan as life changes warrant.

These are our recommendations for using this book:

1. Read and use the book in the order presented.
2. Complete the worksheets as you come to them. You will always be able to return to each worksheet to revise it later if desired, but filling it out while you are most familiar with the subject matter will be helpful.
3. If you are going through the book as an individual, your path is clear and will be guided by the book.
4. If you are going through the book with another person; for example, a partner, family member, or friend, you have a decision to make. There are two options to consider:

a. Each person goes through the steps individually, then compares life plans when they are complete, discusses them, and modifies individual plans to meet shared needs.

b. Go through the steps together while being sensitive to one another's individual needs. We recommend if you choose this approach, that you still develop individual plans.

5. Regardless of how you decide to proceed through the book, make a commitment to yourself to let it make a real difference to your future. Research shows that 90% of those who buy a book like this one either do not finish it or do not follow through on what they have learned. Choose to be in the 10% that will take full advantage of the book to live a full and fulfilling retirement.

One final point—you will find that we will urge you to use written worksheets, plans, and charts. While this may not be what you are most comfortable with, we ask that you give it a try. Research has shown that writing these things down will help you bring them to life. That being said, do what will be most successful for you.

Alan Spector and Keith Lawrence

About LifeScape Solutions™

Alan Spector and Keith Lawrence had been developing the vision for this book for some time. When Bob Miller, Nancy Riesz, Keith, and Alan collaborated to develop LifeScape, LLC, it became the impetus to bring the book to reality. LifeScape added richness to the knowledge that would become the book, and, in its own right, is a holistic retirement planning program developed to meet the growing needs of retiring Baby Boomers. Visit www.LifeScapeRetirement.com.

As LifeScape and *Your Retirement Quest* continued to be developed, we recognized that our retirement planning approach would be valuable to both prospective retirees and their employers. The fastest growing segment of the workforce in the U.S., Europe, and Japan are employees between 55 and 64, many who are delaying retirement because of the economic downturn. Importantly, for these most experienced employees, uncertainty about their future is at the foundation of a trend. They are becoming increasingly distracted and disengaged at work; a trend that is good for neither the employees nor their employers.

As we noted in the Introduction, "Our contention is that one key to reengaging the experienced employee is to create more clarity of vision and a plan for his or her future; years which have the promise of being the best years of his or her life." *Your Retirement Quest* enables individuals to gain greater insight and confidence through the development of their personal and holistic plan; helping them in their "Quest" for a meaningful future. The book and other resources from LifeScape Solutions™, such as "The 3E (Experienced Employee Engagement) Survey," enables employers to rejuvenate the engagement of these extraordinary employees. Our intent is that both the employee and the employer will benefit.

Along with the *10 Secrets for Creating and Living a Fulfilling Retirement*, the basis of moving forward toward a more certain future is the LifeScape Solutions™ model.

LifeScape Solutions™ Model

The model, designed to help you plan for a full and fulfilling retirement, was developed using the best known information and practices and has been successfully shared with future and current retirees in the United States and Europe. This is a brief overview of the model.

Most people go through five stages of retirement: Anticipation, Honeymoon, Disenchantment, and Rejuvenation, represented by the steps leading up the side of the pyramid on the way to the fifth stage, a Fulfilling Retirement.

These are the foundation building blocks and other key elements of the model:

LifeScape Plan: a practical and holistic approach to achieving your dreams in retirement

Well-Being: the energy to live fully today and throughout your retirement

Financial Security: matching your lifestyle to your financial resources

Purpose/Values: your reason for being and what is truly important to you in life

Attitude: the mindset with which you approach life and meet the challenges and opportunities of retirement

Connectedness: initiating and nurturing the many relationships that are important in life

Giving Back: making a valuable contribution to others (friends, family, community, world); being part of something greater than yourself

Passions: activities that give you a sense of energy, provide you with a sense of achievement, and play to your strengths

Growth: being mentally stimulated with new activities, learning, and challenges to keep your life fresh and exciting

Fun: drawing excitement, pleasure, recreation, and satisfaction from life

Alan and Keith's Top Book Recommendations

Branham, Leigh and Hirschfeld, Mark. *Re-Engage: How America's Best Places to Work Inspire Extra Effort in Extraordinary Times.* McGraw-Hill. 2010

> New research and tips on how to fully engage employees from all the generations

Buettner,Dan. *The Blue Zone: Lessons for Living Longer from the People Who Have Lived the Longest.* National Geographic Society. 2008

> How people live in the areas of the world that have the longest life spans

Bufford, Bob. *Halftime: Changing Your Game Plan From Success to Significance.* Zondervan. 1994

> Dealing with the challenge that many men face as they transition their focus from only working to pursuing other dreams in their lives

Fraunfelder, Frederick M.D. & Gilbaugh, James M.D. *Retire Right: 8 Scientifically Proven Traits You Need for a Happy, Fulfilling Retirement.* Avery. 2008

> An overview of many areas two doctors have found to be critical to living a healthy and fulfilling life in retirement

Gambone, James V. *Refirement: The Boomers Guide to Life After 50.* Kirkhouse Publishers. 2000

> How to redefine retirement by exploding some of the current myths and identifying and actively pursuing your underlying passions

Goldsmith, Marshall. *MOJO: How to Get It, How to Keep It, How to Get It Back if You Lose It*. Hyperion. 2009

 The key characteristics of those activities that ignite your personal *MOJO* and sustain it through the years

Gordon, John. *The Energy Addict: 101 Physical, Mental & Spiritual Ways to Energize Your Life*. Perigee Books. 2003

 Valuable insights and "easy to do" ways to dramatically increase your personal energy as well as enjoy life to the fullest

Lyubomirsky, Sonja. *The How of Happiness: The Scientific Approach to Getting The Life You Want*. Penguin Press. 2007

 The keys to what drives happiness and new insights into what really matters in influencing your personal happiness

McCarthy, Kevin. *On Purpose Person: Making Your Life Make Sense*. Pinon Press. 1992

 Discovering and defining your life purpose, your "true north," and how to live it every day

Nash, Laura & Howard Stevenson. *Just Enough: Tools for Creating Success in Your Work & Life*. John Wiley &Sons, Inc. 2004

 A breakthrough way to redefine and expand your definition of personal purpose to incorporate what really counts in sustaining success and happiness

Rentsch, Gail. *Smart Women Don't Retire: They Break Free*. Springboard Press. 2008

 Keen insights into the unique challenges women face as they transition from lifetime careers to what is next in their lives—with practical advice to successfully address them

Roizen, Michael F. M.D. & Oz, Mohmet M.D. *You Staying Young*. Free Press. 2007

 Prominent doctors provide a wide array of practical advice on how to improve and maintain your health and well-being

Schwartz, Tony. *The Way We're Working Isn't Working: The Four Forgotten Needs That Energize Great Performance.* Free Press. 2010

Practical tips from the leader of *The Energy Project* on how to enhance your personal energy and capability to perform at your best and to live an extraordinary life

Ulrich, Dave and Wendy. *The Why of Work: How Great Leaders Build Abundant Organizations.* McGraw Hill. 2010

Insights from thought leaders in the Human Resources field on how to create meaning and abundance at work

Werner, Ralph. *Get A Life: You Don't Need A Million To Retire Well.* Nolo Publishing. 2004

Explodes the myth that you need to be rich to retire successfully and presents what is really most important in your later years

Wuorio, Jeffrey T. *The Complete Idiots Guide to Retirement Planning.* Alpha Press. 2007

How to think and plan your financial security in a multitude of areas (investments, estates, taxes, etc)

Alan and Keith's Top Web Site Recommendations

Blue Zones Vitality Compass (www.bluezones.com)

> Calculate your current biological age based on your daily habits, future life expectancy, and what you can do to live a longer, healthier life

CNN Money (www.money.cnn.com/retirement)

> To help you think through aspects of financial security

Discover Life Purpose (www.knowyourpurpose.com/change)

> To help you define your life's purpose as well as live it every day

Encore Careers (www.encore.org)

> Guidance regarding possible new career opportunities

LifeScape Retirement (www.lifescaperetirement.com)

> Details the LifeScape Solutions™ model and overall program for retirement planning

Lumosity (www.lumosity.com)

> Tools to help you keep your mind sharp and have a lot of fun

Mindtools (www.mindtools.com)

> Practical tools and tips to strengthen your planning skills

StickK (www.stickK.com)

> A tool to help you set clear goals and successfully implement them

Values (www.values.com)

> Helps you clarify your personal values and better apply them in your life

Your Retirement Quest (www.YourRetirementQuest.com)

> Detailed information about this book and LifeScape Solutions™

About the Authors

Alan Spector   *Keith Lawrence*

Alan Spector retired from a 33-year career with the Procter & Gamble Company in 2002, as Director of Worldwide Quality Assurance. In retirement, Alan has pursued two of the passions of his youth, baseball and books; continuing to play senior baseball and having written and published two previous books. He also does volunteer consulting for and serves on the boards of non-profits, works out daily, teaches classes at the elementary and high school levels, writes a weekly Featured Classmate article for his high school class, and is a founding partner of LifeScape Solutions™. Alan and his wife, Ann, live in St. Louis, enjoy their four grandchildren, and travel extensively to visit family, play baseball, and sightsee.

Keith Lawrence had been preparing for over a decade for his retirement from Procter& Gamble in December 2009, as a Director of Human Resources. Keith is a student of peak performance; seeking to learn and teach others how individuals, teams and organizations achieve and sustain success throughout life. He has worked with people from around the world, including partnering with companies such as Toyota, IBM, GE, Staples, Right Management, Accenture, The Energy Project, and the RBL Group, has published several articles and spoken at numerous forums, is a member of several boards and advisory councils, and is a founding partner of LifeScape Solutions™. Keith and his wife, Sue, live in Cincinnati, where he enjoys the flexibility to pursue his life purpose of "unleashing dreams," spending time with their children, dear friends, and other family, traveling more, maintaining his well-being, and giving back to others to make the world a better place.

ORDER Your Retirement Quest

Your Retirement Quest is available directly from the publisher at

www.cincybooks.com

Order quantity: _____ copies at $18.95 per book

Postage & handling: $4.00 for 1 book and $2.00 for each additional book being shipped to the same address. Shipping to multiple addresses is $4.00 per book.

Book Subtotal $ _____

Postage & Handling $ _____

Sales Tax (Ohio only) $ _____ ($1.42/book)

Total Amount Due $ _____

For quantity purchases and discount information for ten (10) or more books, contact Alan Spector: Alan@YourRetirementQuest.com

Enclosed is my ( ) check   ( ) money order
Please charge my
( ) Visa   ( ) MasterCard   ( ) Discover   ( ) American Express

Card # _____Expiration date _____

Signature as on card _____

Name _____

Address _____

City _____State _____ Zip _____

For more information about the book or about LifeScape Solutions™ seminars, visit **www.YourRetirementQuest.com**